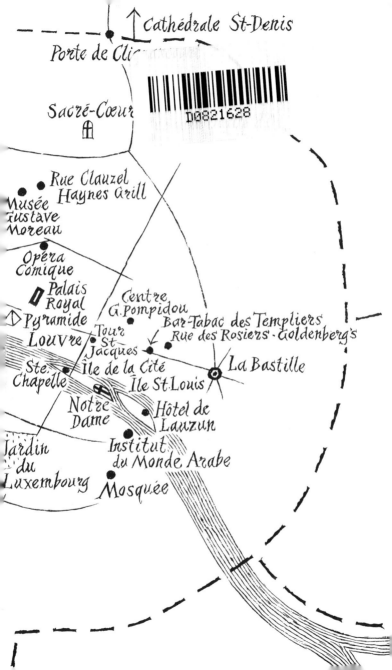

The Flâneur

BY THE SAME AUTHOR

The Married Man
Marcel Proust
The Farewell Symphony
The Beautiful Room is Empty
Nocturnes for the King of Naples
Skinned Alive
The Burning Library
Genet
Caracole
Forgetting Elena
States of Desire: Travels in Gay America
Sketches from Memory: People and Places in the
Heart of Our Paris

The Flâneur

A Stroll through the
Paradoxes of Paris

Edmund White

BLOOMSBURY

First published 2001

Copyright © 2001 by Edmund White

The moral right of the author has been asserted

Bloomsbury Publishing Plc,
38 Soho Square, London WID 3HB

A CIP catalogue record for this book
is available from the British Library

ISBN 0 7475 4957 5

10 9 8 7 6 5 4 3 2 1

Typeset by Hewer Text Ltd, Edinburgh
Printed by Clays Ltd, St Ives plc

ACKNOWLEDGEMENTS

The author gratefully acknowledges Michael Carroll's editorial suggestions and loving support, Liz Calder's patience, Catherine Lupton's research skills and Jean-Jacques Aillagon's generosity in opening previously closed doors. Marie-Claude de Brunhoff has given constant encouragement and very concrete help. It is she who has accompanied every step in the author's Paris wanderings over the last twenty years.

To Marilyn Schaefer, my favourite *flâneur*

If I were to say, as I believe, that kindliness is the distinguishing characteristic of Parisians, I am afraid I should offend them. 'I don't want to be kind!'

Stendhal, Love

'I've been thinking, I should have come back to Canada with you as another distressed Canadian.'

'But you wouldn't. You were in love with Paris. You thought it was the Great Good Place. Well, it's not. You were in love with a dream.'

I see he was right. It was a dream of excellence and beauty, one that does not exist anywhere in real life. Montparnasse and its people came very close to it. But no city or society in the world, even the Paris of those days, can realize the elusive dream I had.

John Glassco, Memoirs of Montparnasse

Having lived in Paris unfits you for living anywhere, including Paris.

John Ashbery (quoted in
The Last Avant-Garde by David Lehman)

CHAPTER ONE

PARIS IS A BIG CITY, in the sense that London and New York are big cities and that Rome is a village, Los Angeles a collection of villages and Zürich a backwater.

A reckless friend defines a big city as a place where there are blacks, tall buildings and you can stay up all night. By that definition Paris is deficient in tall buildings; although President Pompidou had a scheme in the sixties and early seventies to fill Paris with skyscrapers, he succeeded only in marring the historic skyline with the faulty towers of a branch university, Paris VII at Jussieu (which was recently closed because it was copiously insulated with asbestos), the appalling Tour Montparnasse – and the bleak wasteland of the office district, La Défense.

La Défense has few apartment dwellers other

than Africans and the rootless, whereas the young white middle class for whom it was intended are all off living in the restored Marais district with its exposed beams and period fireplaces. La Défense went directly from being futuristic to being passé without ever seeming like a normal feature of the present.

Honestly, instead of 'like a normal feature of the present' I almost wrote 'without ever being inscribed within the interior of the present'. That's how much I've been submerged in contemporary French nonfiction. I frequently have to stop and ask myself how a human being might put the same idea. When I was young in the 1950s and 60s, college-age Americans with intellectual pretensions made the pilgrimage to St Germain, the Sorbonne and such Left Bank nightclubs as La Rose Rouge (young gays chose a different colour, La Reine Blanche). The quickness of Parisian thought and especially its authoritative tone thoroughly intimidated young foreigners of every nationality in those days – and I was one of them. Americans had the additional thrill of being despised, since nearly 40 per cent of the French populace (and virtually all intellectuals) still voted Communist. The hatred was not reciprocated. Americans had always loved Paris; one French study, *Paris dans la littérature américaine* by Jean Meral, lists two hundred American novels about Paris written between 1824 and 1978.

In the 1950s American and British students admired and read Sartre and Camus and, if they were religious, Merleau-Ponty because their own philosophers back home had dismissed all metaphysical and most moral questions as either nonsense or irrelevant to philosophy's true concerns. Romantic young people, of course, turn to philosophy for nothing but a metaphysical chill or a moral conflagration. The prevailing school of language philosophy in the English-speaking world presented little to stir the soul or fire the imagination of young Romantics. French philosophy, on the other hand, was involving because it was sternly ethical: the individual was responsible for all his actions and through the least concession to convenience or smugness could easily start living a lie and fall into the dreaded pit of *mauvaise foi*. All writers and thinkers everywhere, moreover, were called on to play a role in society, to be *engagé* or 'committed'.

Paris's role as a generator of ideas, as well as of manners and fads and fashions, also contributes to its status as a big city. Small cities don't set standards in international morality, not as Paris has done since the eighteenth century when *les philosophes* redefined the social contract and Voltaire defended a convicted criminal named Jean Calas who he was convinced was innocent. Voltaire was right and succeeded in clearing Calas' name and winning Paris a worldwide reputation as a place where justice would triumph – at least if a famous writer could be convinced to embrace the cause. A century later the novelist Émile Zola proved the rule by taking up the trampled banner of Alfred Dreyfus, a Jewish officer in the French army who'd been convicted by an anti-Semitic military court of selling secrets to Germany. In 1894 Dreyfus was sent off to Devil's Island, French Guiana; he was freed and eventually rehabilitated only years later – after Zola reopened the case in the press. (An image of his famous front-page newspaper article 'J'Accuse!', an open letter to the President of the Republic, was projected in its entirety on the front of the National Assembly on the night of 13 January 1998, commemorating the centennial of the historical event.)

I suppose the two stories could be interpreted more as testimonials to the importance of writers in French culture than as evidence of French justice. Certainly the English-speaking world has never observed anything like the novelist

Jean Genet's trial in 1943 for repeated convictions as a thief. Genet faced life imprisonment as punishment for his recidivism, but Jean Cocteau, who had discovered Genet and arranged to publish his first novel, *Our Lady of the Flowers*, submitted a statement read out in court: 'He is Rimbaud, one cannot condemn Rimbaud.' He suggested that the judge might go down in history as a philistine if he made the wrong decision. Not for a moment did Cocteau argue that Genet was innocent, simply that he was a genius. His testimony got Genet off scot-free.

These exemplary – even startling – cases should be weighed against the peremptory, often arrogant justice handed out to ordinary citizens. There is no *habeas corpus* in France and until recently perfectly innocent people could be held for months, even years, in preventive detention if a judge thought they knew more than they were saying. As Mavis Gallant wrote of the judge in France, 'He is free to hold you until you change your mind. If you turn out to be innocent, you have no recourse against the law. You cannot even sue for the symbolic one franc in damages, though preventive detention may have cost you your job, your domestic equilibrium and your reputation.' In the 1960s, in the wake of the Algerian War, hundreds of Arabs languished in

Edmund White

French prisons for long periods, though they'd
never been tried, much less convicted.

But I've given enough serious, intellectual (even
negative) reasons for defining Paris as a big city.
There are many more minor ones, including the
fact that it's a place where you can sleep all day if
you want to, score heroin, hear preposterous
theories that are closely held and furiously argued (especially in the 'philosophical cafés',
where meetings are regularly scheduled to discuss
ethical questions). In Paris you can encounter
genuine tolerance of other races and religions –
and of atheism. It is a city where you can swap
your wife if you want to – indoors, in a special
club called Chris and Manu's, or in your own car
outdoors near the Porte Dauphine (where you
can enjoy the additional thrill of exhibitionism,
since male voyeurs lurk around the parked and
locked automobiles and stare into the steamed-
over windows). Paris is a city where even the
most outrageous story of incest and murder is
greeted with a verbal shrug: '*Mais c'est normal!*'
  It's true that Paris is made up of equal parts of
social conservatism and anarchic experimenta-
tion, but foreigners never quite know where to
place the moral accent mark. At least it's certain
we're always mistaken if we attempt to predict

the response of *le français moyen* (the average French person, if such a creature exists). The French can be as indignant as a Texas Baptist over stories of men who buy child pornography; in the early nineties the names of a ring of such men were published in the national newspapers, which led to several suicides. There was no distinction made between those who staged the pornography and those who bought it, nor between films about prepubescent children and those about teenagers.

On the other hand, no one in Paris would worry about presidential sex affairs and the only doubt most people have about Lionel Jospin is that he's too Protestant to have a mistress. Mitterrand's illegitimate daughter Mazarine enjoyed a brief moment of widespread popularity after her father's death until she did something really dubious and published a mediocre novel. Certainly the fuss in America over Monica Lewinsky's 'White House knee pads', as she called them, made the French hold their sides with continental mirth and superior erotic sophistication.

Nonsexual political corruption used to be shrugged off with a similar Gallic weariness, but the whole Latin world, eager to build the new 'Europe' with Germany, the Netherlands and Scandinavia, has been cleaning up its act.

Even so, most trials of high government officials in France (whether for deporting Jews during the war or paying one's own wife the equivalent of $40,000 for preparing a ten-page report or failing to screen the blood bank for the AIDS virus) end not with a bang but with a whimper. One day you realize that you haven't heard about a given scandal for a long time. Since the newspapers have no tradition of hard-hitting investigative reporting, inertia is allowed to bury even last year's hottest story in the great compost heap that the French call *le non-dit* – the 'unsaid'.

I suppose the most basic index of any city's big-cityness is what you can find in it. In Paris you can find Tex-Mex food served in a courtyard surrounded by a dance rehearsal space (Le Studio): you eat your tamales tranquilly while looking up at dancers in practice clothes lunging and twirling behind fogged-over windows. You can rent a whole castle for an American-style Hallowe'en party (at least we rented the château of Château Maisons-Laffite one year, with disastrous results, since the French showed up not as witches and monsters but as marquis and marquises). Now Hallowe'en has become the newest national fête. You can visit not one but *two* copies of the Statue of Liberty – one in a shaded corner of the Luxembourg Gardens and the other in the middle of the Seine between the fifteenth and sixteenth arrondissements on the Pont de Grenelle. You can find seventeen vegetarian restaurants, even though Parisians roll their eyes to heaven when Americans begin with their weird food fetishes, their cult of whole grain or fermented seaweed or no sugar or butter. You can find not one but several places to go ballroom dancing at five in the afternoon on a Tuesday, say; I've been to the Balajo on the rue de Lapp and to the Java on the rue Faubourg du Temple. At the Java I remember big peroxided retired waitresses being swooped and dipped by tiny black African salesmen of a certain age (and finesse!). A slightly nutty friend of mine in his twenties claimed that he used to go to the *thé dansant* every afternoon at a major restaurant on the Boulevard Montparnasse where elderly ladies sent drinks to young gigolos, who then asked them to dance. During a spin across the basement floor some interesting arrangements were worked out; my friend went home with one dowager and cleaned her apartment wearing nothing but a starched apron – and earned a thousand francs.

In Paris you can visit the sewers and the catacombs. You can meet collectors of Barbie dolls. You can go to a Buddhist centre in the Bois de Vincennes (strangely, the buildings were originally designed for the Colonial Exposition of 1931 as the pavilions for Togo and the Cameroons). You can visit a wax museum, the Musée Grevin, where chic people sometimes give private parties in the miniature theatre filled with likenesses of Rudolf Nureyev and Pavarotti. You can go to a restaurant that serves just caviar or another that serves just cheese. You can visit Russian *izbas* (log houses) that were originally constructed in the mid-nineteenth century for an international fair until they were transplanted to a quiet neighbourhood, where they still stand, ignored by everyone.

When I first started living in Paris in the early 1980s there were still knife sharpeners, glaziers and chimney sweeps strolling the streets, each with his distinctive cry. The chimney sweeps still exist, though most of them are crooks who present phoney papers and demand lots of money for an ineffectual swipe at your fireplace. *Le petit ramoneur* may be a classic figure in the Parisian erotic imagination, though unfortunately he can no longer be counted on to unclog more intimate pipes.

In Paris you can find a large bird market on the Île de la Cité on Sundays and you can also attend a Mass in Latin in a creepy right-wing church off the

Place Maubert where the priests have been ex-
communicated for not adhering to Vatican re-
forms and the members of the parish all look
and act like Stepford wives and husbands. You
can find a market for second-hand and rare books
in the outlying area of Vanves under a large, open-
sided glass and metal awning. It offers the collector the equivalent of a city block of books. You
can wander for hours through the world's most
luxurious flea market completely on the other side
of Paris at Clignancourt. In the very centre of the
vast Clignancourt maze is a restaurant serving
sausage and greasy fries where all the waiters
and waitresses take turns singing like the French
cabaret stars of the past; the proprietress reserves
for herself an exclusive on Piaf. With her brightly
painted, perfectly maintained red nails she makes
sweeping gestures up and down the length of her
body, confident, stylized gestures at odds with her
ringed, tormented eyes.

Of course Paris is the shopping city *par excellence*. Women who want to be dressed by
couturiers can still find them in Paris if they're
willing to pay up to $35,000 for a frock.
Although nearly half of all Parisians are content
to appear neat and anonymous, the rest make
some effort to follow fashions. One year, for
instance, every man will be dressed in a silk

jacket, another year in sherbert-coloured summer linens. In the eighties many women wore the gaudy, Provençal-inspired Christian La Croix prints; miniskirts were in and women of every age and size could be seen tugging at them as they slid into a car or pressing their knees together and twisting them to one side as they sat on stage during a TV broadcast or a conference. (The Avenue Foch is both the home of Paris's millionaires, who live in stadium-size apartments, and of *poules de luxe*, those upscale whores who stand in the doorways. When La Croix first emerged as a leading designer a rich friend of mine sailed out of her Avenue Foch apartment in her gaudy miniskirt. The local *pute* said timidly, 'Excuse me, madam. That's such a lovely dress. Who designed it?' My friend said grandly, 'La Croix. *Haute couture*, of course.' The prostitute appeared in the same dress on her beat the next night.)

The French invented the idea of *luxe* and have always been willing to pay for it or, short of that, find cheap, clever rip-offs. A ritual of Parisian life is trading *les bonnes adresses* – the names and locations of some talented upholsterer or hatmaker or re-caner of straw-bottomed chairs or of a lovely little neighbourhood seamstress. Or the best places for buying whatever details of home decoration that will prove one is *à la page*: the alabaster obelisk for the desk or the ostrich eggs for the coffee table or the lapis lazuli miniature sphinx or the yellow bear lamps lit from within for the children's bedroom.

Above a certain level of income and social standing every detail in a life follows a fad. For a while everyone had to serve dinner in the kitchen, which meant entirely redecorating the kitchen so that it would be Philippe Starck sleek and preparing nothing but cold food. The French have a horror of the smell of cooking food, whereas Americans find it appetizing; in the nineteenth century the first French Rothschild went so far in this aversion as to have the food brought from the kitchen to the dining room on an odourless, because underground, train.

Of course following fads means avoiding those that are already too successful. Recently I attended a dinner where a group of five sophisticated gay men (a furniture designer, a right-wing journalist, a building manager, a trade-fair organizer and a sculptor) all talked about '*l'air du temps*'. I was hazy about the expression, but I knew they couldn't have meant Nina Ricci's perfume. I finally realized it must mean something like *Zeitgeist*, the ideas or fashions that are in the air and stronger than the taste of any one person. They were all deploring the way that in spite of their best efforts '*l'air du temps*' affected their own aesthetic decisions. Naming a shop on the rue du Faubourg St Honoré that features objects of all sorts and changes them constantly, the sculptor said, 'I go by Colette's all the time just to see what *l'air du temps* consists of – that way I can avoid it.' The furniture designer added, 'Taste is something you will and choose, *l'air du temps* is completely involuntary.'

In Paris you can buy anything. At Izrael's Le Monde des Epices you can find tequila and tacos, pancake mix and black-eyed peas, popcorn in heat-and-serve silver foil bags and the best plum slivovitz. There are four major English-language bookshops (the most *sympathique* is the Village Voice at 6 rue Princesse on the Left Bank), two or three for the German language, one in Catalan and Spanish – and two French bookshops that sell nothing but old Jules Verne books in the original bindings. Fauchon, the famous grocer and caterer on the Place Madeleine, offers Skippy's peanut butter, not to mention all the edible delights the mind can imagine or remember, including a pale-green pistachio cake. In a Japanese women's shop around the corner from the Village Voice you can find the soaps and perfumes produced in Florence by the *farmacia* attached to Santa Maria Novella; the *farmacia* has been in business since the seventeenth century. The best silver (Puiforcat), the best sheets (Noel and Pourthault), the best florist (Lachaume, in business since Proust's day, or Christian Tortu near the Odéon for something more up to date) . . . Oh, it's all there – except a truly refined and elegant Italian meal (the French think all the Italians eat is pizza). The other thing that is missing is a decent public library system. There's no library that has open stacks for browsers – that paradise of intellectual serendipity.

The variety of Paris is matched by the energy, the voraciousness and passion of its population. Balzac observed that the appetites for gold and pleasure were so strong in Paris that its citizens quickly burned themselves out. 'In Paris there are only two ages,' he wrote, 'youth and decay; a bloodless, pallid youth and a decay painted to seem youthful.' He also took note of the Parisians' love of novelty – and their devotion to nothing. Or, as he put it:

The Parisian is interested in everything and, in the end, interested in nothing . . . Intoxicated as he is with something new from one day to the next, the Parisian, regardless of age, lives like a child. He complains of everything, tolerates everything, mocks everything, forgets everything, desires everything, tastes everything, feels everything passionately, drops everything casually – his kings, his conquests, his glory, his idol, whether made of bronze or glass . . .

Since Balzac's day, of course, Paris has changed. No one is too ambitious, since its populace is now cosseted in the meagre but constant comforts of the socialist state, and the city's glory days are long in the past. But the passion for novelty still reigns. Perhaps Paris is the one city left where the tyranny of Paris fashions still holds women in its thrall. A great theatre director, a perfume, a new fad – all will be embraced one season and forgotten the next. There is nothing more final or frightening than the way a Parisian hisses out the words '*C'est fini! ça? c'est dépassé, c'est démodé.*' Even children say it with ruthless confidence.

And no wonder Paris, land of novelty and distraction, is the great city of the *flâneur* – that aimless stroller who loses himself in the crowd, who has no destination and goes wherever caprice or curiosity directs his or her steps. In New York the stroller can amble along from the Wall Street area up through SoHo, the East and West Village and Chelsea, but then he must hop a cab up to Amsterdam and Columbus on the Upper West Side; the rest of the city is a desert.

In Paris virtually every district is beautiful, alluring and full of unsuspected delights, especially those that fan out around the Seine in the first through the eighth arrondissements. This is the classic Paris, defined by the Arc de Triomphe and the Eiffel Tower to the west and the Bastille and the Panthéon to the east. Everything within this magic parallelogram is worth visiting on foot, starting with the two river islands, the Île de la Cité and the Île St Louis, and working one's way up the Boulevard St Germain from the Île St Louis to the heart of St-Germain-des-Prés, with its trio of famous establishments, the Lipp restaurant and the twin cafés, the Flore and Les Deux Magots.

In 1939 Léon-Paul Fargue could write without a hint of irony:

If during the day there was an English cabinet meeting, a boxing match in the state of New Jersey, a First Prize for Conformism, a literary punch in the ribs, a contest for tenors on the Right Bank or a nasty squabble, the habitués of the cafés on the Place St-Germain-des-Prés would be among the first to be affected by the results of these meetings or competitions. The square in fact lives, breathes, palpitates and sleeps by virtue of three cafés as famous today as State institutions.

For Fargue the third café was the Royal St-Germain, but he might as well have included the Brasserie Lipp, across the street from the Flore, where in the 1930s *le Tout-Paris politique* lunched or dined.

This square has undoubtedly lost some of its intellectual lustre. Everyone is lamenting the boutiquification of St-Germain-des-Prés, and it's true that one of the best bookstores, Le Divan, has been replaced by Dior, that one of the few record stores in the area has been cannibalized by Cartier, and Le Drugstore – a late-night complex of tobacco stand, restaurant and chemist – has been supplanted by Armani. Louis Vuitton has installed a chic shop right next to Les Deux Magots.

OK, the move of Le Divan, which had been in the same place since its opening in 1921, to the outer Siberia of the *petit-bourgeois* fifteenth arrondissement really does spell a major loss to St Germain des Prés and seriously compromises its intellectual pretensions. It was a bookshop (founded by Henri Martineau, a publisher who lived above the premises) where, incredibly, the staff were *friendly* and where the dusty window displays might be devoted to turn-of-the-century epigrammatic poets from Mauritius or to the previously unpublished madhouse rants of Antonin Artaud, dashed off after a particularly vigorous electroshock session. No cookbooks or slimming manuals, nothing to help in planning that next vacation or home improvement. Nothing but difficult literature and austere volumes of theory and philosophy. Fortunately, a very similar and even larger bookstore, La Hune, is just around the corner and usually open to midnight, even if the salespeople are a bit more *timides* (French for 'rude').

I can't see why people are lamenting the disappearance of Le Drugstore, a sordid mini-mall for those overcome at midnight with a low (and more wisely repressed) urge to buy Gitanes or Otis Redding tapes or bottles of Habit Rouge. It used to be a place where rent boys lounged about during a thunderstorm, but in recent years it hasn't even had that excuse for existing. The record store across the street simply couldn't compete with the giant book–CD–booking-agent–camera-store complex just up the rue de Rennes, the FNAC. And Vuitton did nothing more heinous than take over half of an old jewellery store called Arthus-Bertrand, a place so traditional that it supplies members of the

French Academy with their swords. (I once met Arthus-Bertrand *fils*, who explained to me that he had a job more difficult than any diplomat's. Apparently the friends and admirers of a new academician get up a fund to purchase the sword, but the nominee never knows the exact sum. When the future academician comes into the shop to choose his sword, it's the young proprietor's awkward job to steer him away from the diamonds for his hilt towards these lovely zircons just over here. Now at least he can stop worrying about the high overhead, since Vuitton is footing half the bill.)

No, there's no denying that St-Germain is no longer Intelligence Central for the whole world as it once claimed to be. What made St-Germain famous internationally was the artists and philosophers just before, during and after the Second World War. In those days intellectuals and artists usually lived in hotels – dingy, crowded, underheated little furnished rooms – and went to cafés to eat, drink, work, socialize and stay warm. As Jean-Paul Sartre, that high priest of Existentialism, recalled, he and Simone de Beauvoir 'more or less set up house in the Flore' in 1940:

> We worked from 9 a.m. till noon, when we went out to lunch. At 2 we came back and talked with

our friends till four, when we got down to work
again till eight. And after dinner people came to
see us by appointment. It may seem strange, all
this, but the Flore was like home to us: even when
the air-raid alarm went off we would merely
feign to leave and then climb up to the first floor
and go on working . . .

It wasn't all work and intellectual chat, however.
As Beauvoir recalls, there were also scores of idle
young people who 'were very, very bored'.

But the offices of most of the major publishing
houses were nearby, the Sorbonne was a fifteen-
minute walk away in one direction, and in the
other there was the Chambre des Députés, the
equivalent to the House of Commons. In St-
Germain juries met to hand out literary prizes,
movie deals were put together – and Sartre was
introduced to Jean Genet for the first time on the
terrace of Les Deux Magots. Le Corbusier, Gia-
cometti, Picasso and the American Surrealist
photographer Man Ray all hung out in St-Germain, partly because it was also near many of the
galleries. Nightclubs such as La Rose Rouge and
Le Tabou introduced bebop and *le jazz hot*.

Above all, pale young women all in black and
their gaunt boyfriends in turtlenecks were pre-
senting themselves to the passing tourists as

Existentialists, which seemed mainly a matter of despairing conspicuously, carrying around a volume of *Being and Nothingness*, listening to Juliette Greco songs and drinking lots of cognacs. Albert Camus, looking as good as one possibly can in one of those fattening trenchcoats; Françoise Sagan, looking like a child whose puppy has just died; Alexander Calder, looking like an awakened owl – these were just some of the denizens of this celebrated neighbourhood.

If St-Germain is now less interesting, it's because Paris itself has become a cultural backwater. There aren't more than two or three internationally known French painters living anywhere in France (I'm being generous, since there's really only one, Christian Boltanski, and a young sculptor, Jean-Michel Othoniel); the galleries look like amateur art fairs, all palette-knife landscapes and sad-faced children; few French novels are translated into other languages; since Foucault's death no philosopher has had a universal stature; the centre of the city is too expensive to welcome young bohemians or wannabe novelists, who've all fled to Prague or Budapest, even Riga. London, New York, Berlin and Tokyo are the happening capitals. French culture has become a museum and the sizeable arts budget goes mainly to what is lugubriously named *le patrimoine*. Even the Paris club scene is so dismal that every weekend the 'E-crowd' is tunnelling its way over to London.

As a result, St-Germain-des-Prés is free to give up its quirky, independent, arty status and to join up with the surrounding luxury of the Faubourg St-Germain, that stately world of imposing eighteenth-century *hôtels particuliers* where Proust's aristocratic hostesses once reigned, the Paris of embassies and *haute couture*. It's sort of as though a beatnik brat has grown up to be an elegant and rather brainless matron.

From St-Germain I like to work my way down the rue Bonaparte past the furniture and fabric stores, the Académie des Beaux Arts and the shops selling prints, finishing at the Institute, the building that houses the French Academy and its library, the Bibliothèque Mazarine. In front of the Institute, which is my favourite structure in Paris for the nobility of its dome and its perfect, Italianate proportions, is a wooden footbridge that leads over to the Louvre and its Cour Carré, which at night is lit so ingeniously that it floats above the few visitors like some calm, wise, idealized vision of itself – a gushing fountain in the centre, the walls adorned with bas reliefs by Jean Goujon – and through the central arch sparkles a glimpse of the illuminated, icy sides of I. M. Pei's glass pyramid.

From there I like to go to the Palais Royal, an oasis of silence and elegance in the heart of the old city. Once you get past the tacky silver balls or the striped columns by Buren, you're back in the world of Colette and Cocteau, the two most famous denizens of the Palais in the twentieth century. They were neighbours and could wave to one another from their windows. Colette liked to look at Cocteau in his low-ceilinged entresol apartment lit from below by the sunlight bouncing up from the pavement, as though he were an actor illuminated by footlights.

Immobilized by arthritis, Colette seldom stirred from her bed during her last years. She'd sit under the shade she'd fashioned out of a piece of her signature blue writing paper, snug under her fur pelisses and attended by her faithful last – and much younger – husband.

Colette was full of contradictions. She despised feminists and said that the only things they deserved were the lash and the harem, but she herself divorced twice, lived openly as a lesbian for a decade, danced half-naked on the stage at the turn of the century and had an affair with her teenage stepson when she was approaching fifty. She turned her own mother into an endearing character, 'Sido', and presented her to the public with convincing filial piety, but in real life she ignored her during her long decline and refused to attend her funeral. Colette was famously kind to cats and liked to picture herself as someone so close to nature she was almost feral, but in actuality she quite unnaturally rejected and ridiculed her own daughter, left her in the care of servants, then packed her off to strict boarding schools. Finally, Colette's third and last husband was a Jew whom she adored and managed to save from harm during the Nazi Occupation, but she contributed to collaborationist magazines and in 1941 she published a novel, *Julie de Carneilhan*, full of anti-Semitic slurs. Chapters of it came out in *Gringoire*, a collaborationist review (in her issue there was a cartoon of 'Uncle Sem' and one of the Statue of Liberty wearing a menorah). And though she was quintessentially French and regarded as a national treasure, the Catholic Church refused to give her a religious funeral.

Of course, what this summary omits is her genius, which made many people want to forgive her all her shortcomings. She was generally considered to be the leading French woman novelist from the mid-1920s, when her talent emerged in all its glory, till her death at the age of eighty-one in 1954; now we would say she was, after the death of Proust in 1922, quite simply the most talented French novelist of her epoch, male or female. Although other writers, mostly male, spoke of her as an entirely unconscious writer guided only by her instincts, in fact Colette constantly revised her manuscripts, always searching for an exact, even shocking image.

Perhaps what confused critics was her originality. She claimed, with some justice, that she owed nothing to any preceding writer. In general French literature from the seventeenth century on has favoured short sentences, a narrow vocabulary of unremarkable words and a strict limit on metaphorical excess. Ironically, however, the two biggest literary figures of the century in France have turned out to be among the least characteristic – Proust and Colette. If Proust wrote extremely long sentences, unparalleled in contemporary French prose, Colette had an equally unidiomatic affection for strange words (she has the largest vocabulary in modern French) and for highly coloured imagery.

Along with Proust, Colette experimented with the first-person narrator, someone clearly based on herself but whom she both conceals and reveals in book after book and indisputably *constructs*. Like Proust, who used his narrator as a *fil conducteur* to draw us through his thousands of pages, Colette coquettishly suggests and subtracts details about herself in her entire nearly eighty-volume *oeuvre* of fiction, memoirs, journalism and drama.

The French today are slightly confused by how seriously English-speaking readers take Colette, a writer they think of as someone their grandmothers read under the hairdryer (during her own lifetime she fared much better). Perhaps their underevaluation of Colette is linked to the fact that few women novelists, other than George Sand and Colette, dominated French literature in the long period before Yourcenar and Beauvoir; the French don't happen to have the equivalent to Jane Austen and George Eliot. Moreover, Colette's lurid image as one of those seedy old Decadents – friend to Rachilde (author of *Monsieur Venus*), Proust's mentor Robert de Montesquiou and the *grandes cocottes* Liane de Pougy and la Belle Otéro, mistresses of kings – clings to her in her land of origin. That in her lifetime she wrote constant articles for the press, posed for photographers as a mummy or a man, was whispered about in gossip columns, and even opened a chain of beauty salons (from which her clients emerged looking fifteen years older, according to Natalie Barney), all proved to her compatriots that she wasn't a serious person. Her case was analogous to that of Proust, who was dismissed at first because he had written about society events for *Le Figaro*.

In fact one can make a good case that only foreigners can properly judge a contemporary – distance gives the objectivity that time will eventually provide even to compatriots. Or, as the French sociologist and philosopher Pierre Bourdieu puts it more elegantly, 'Foreign judgements are a little like the judgements of posterity.' Just as the French were the first critics to praise Faulkner, just as Americans from the first admired Virginia Woolf and ignored her offputting Bloomsbury connections, in the same way Colette has always been esteemed in the English-speaking world more than at home.

For us Colette is not only a perverse, sometimes stern sensualist, she is also *the* great nature writer, who brings cats, dogs, plants, even the soil sharply into focus. And she is, in spite of herself, a feminist in the only way that makes sense in fiction – she shows a huge variety of women, victimized and monstrous, abject and proud, dependent and supremely resourceful. Even militant feminists have shown less of the range of female experience. Finally, she is the author of half a dozen masterpieces – *Chéri* and *The Last of*

Chéri, *The Pure and the Impure*, *Break of Day*, *My Mother's House* and *Sido* – and the libretto for Ravel's exquisite one-act opera *L'Enfant et les sortilèges*.

Colette – or, to give her her full name, Sidonie-Gabrielle Colette – was born on 28 January 1873 in the Burgundian village of St-Sauveur-en-Puisaye. Her mother, known as Sido or Sidonie, was a freethinker and atheist – not the usual French villager of the period. She had married a rich madman known in the region as the Ape. After his death she married a second time, for love – an amiable but spendthrift Captain Colette, who gradually dissipated the fortune she'd inherited from the Ape. The Captain was as kindly as he was impractical; his leg had been amputated in 1859 after a war wound, and in his later years he had what amounted to a sinecure: he was the tax collector of St-Sauveur.

But the family had its secrets. Sido's ancestors had converted to Protestanism in the seventeenth century and emigrated to Martinique, where they'd acquired slaves. Their children were biracial, a fact the family back in France hid by faking identity papers. Like Pushkin and Dumas, Colette turns out to be of mixed African descent. (Colette herself was proud of her black heritage and frequently referred to it in letters to friends.)

In the summer of 1889, when she was sixteen, Colette fell in love with a thirty-year-old writer and man-about-Paris, Henry Gauthier-Villars, known as Willy. He can be called a 'writer' only in an honorary sense, given that he had a terrible lifelong writer's block and got the most famous composers of the day to pen his columns as a music critic and hired a team of ghost writers to churn out his many novels. He married the provocative, pretty and wildly clever Colette and soon enough set her to work ghosting 'his' most famous novels, the Claudine series. Years later, when she was in her sixties and still nursing a grudge against her first husband, Colette claimed in her memoirs, *My Apprenticeships*, that she had never been so unhappy as with Willy, but her letters of the period belie her subsequent statements. Even she admitted that Willy had edited her work brilliantly; and from him she must have learned a lot about gender-bending, which would become her great subject. As her most recent biographer, Judith Thurman, puts it, 'Colette's early work is a fascinating and baroque form of transvestism. She is a woman writing as a man, who poses as a boyish girl, Claudine, who marries a "feminized" man, the ageing Renaud, who pushes her into the arms of a female lover, Rézi, with whom she takes the virile role.'

One aspect of Colette's life is how *modern* it sounds to today's reader. She ate sushi at the turn of the century, had a facelift in the 1920s, hired an acupuncturist, kept her wild hair permed her whole life, rejected religion, flouted most of society's rules – and ate with such relish and so little guilt that she ended up weighing 180 pounds. (Once, recovering from food poisoning, Colette soothed her stomach by downing a stuffed cabbage and a currant tart.) She announced that slimness was dangerously 'masculinizing' women. She loved perfumes and sprayed each room with a different scent, attuned to its décor. She was one of the first serious writers to turn to the silent movies and devise scenarios that were neither novelistic nor theatrical but purely cinematic. She was obviously open to anything and everything; once when she had some painful dental work she asked, 'Why can't one simply have one's teeth all pulled and replace them with green jade?'

Colette's second husband, Henry de Jouvenel, was a baron, the editor-in-chief of *Le Matin* and after the First World War France's chief delegate to the League of Nations. He was also the father

of Colette's only child, Colette Renée de Jouvenel, who was born on 3 July 1913, when Colette
was forty. Colette gave the baby the Provençal
nickname her own father had given her – Bel-
Gazou. Not for a moment did Colette let her
child distract her from her work; as Colette
observed with pride (forgetting her objections
to masculine women), 'My strain of virility saved
me from the danger which threatens the writer,
elevated to a happy and tender parent, of becoming a mediocre author . . .' Not that Colette
wasn't fiercely possessive of her daughter; once
when the child fell and hurt herself, her mother
slapped her and shouted, 'I'll teach you to ruin
what I made.' A friend on another occasion had
to tear a whip out of Colette's hand as she was
about to lash her daughter. Bel-Gazou once announced she wanted to convert to Judaism because she'd observed that Jews love their
children.

The daughter, of course, was the one who had
to pay the price for her mother's fierce, complex
feelings. Bel-Gazou grew up to be her mother's
greatest disappointment – a spoiled brat, a bad
student, later incapable of settling down to a
career, chronically indecisive. When she eventually decided that she was a lesbian, her mother
– who incidentally had lived ten years with an-

other woman, the Marquise de Belbeuf, a transvestite better known as Missy – radiated disappointment. According to Colette's friend the novelist Michel del Castillo, 'To be gay, in her view, showed a kind of sexual irresponsibility.'

After Colette's death Bel-Gazou fought for years with her mother's last husband, Maurice Goudeket (who had been sixteen years younger than his wife), to gain control over the literary estate. Despite Colette's perfectly explicit preference for Maurice in her will, the daughter won – and turned herself into a high priestess of the cult of Colette. When she was sixty, eight years before her death, Bel-Gazou recalled that her mother had been a font of 'tenderness and warmth that made me radiant with happiness. And nothing that later came to torment or frustrate me could tarnish that magic.'

The magic still radiates from Colette's apartment on the second floor of number 9 rue de Beaujolais. Today the place, which is just three rooms, belongs to the famous decorator Jacques Grange. I visited him there once to interview him, and he has kept a few of her things, including her portrait by Irving Penn – though he did remove from the ceiling the wallpaper Colette had put up so that when she was in bed she didn't have to look up at a harsh blank white rectangle. He can look down on the gardens of the Palais Royal from the window where Colette, crippled with arthritis, would survey her world.

Paris is a world meant to be seen by the walker alone, for only the pace of strolling can take in all the rich (if muted) detail. The loiterer, the *flâneur*, has a long, distinguished pedigree in France. An Italian traveller said in 1577, 'Looking at people go by has always been the Parisians' favourite pastime; no wonder they're called gawkers.' A few years before the Revolution a writer named Louis Sébastien Mercier wandered the streets of Paris taking notes about the cries of strolling vendors, studying boutiques and watching the hundred and one crafts of the great city being practised. In a massive work called *Picture of Paris* in twelve volumes (published from 1781 to 1789), Mercier argued for wider streets (with sidewalks and latrines) and called for an improvement in the desperate lot of the poor.

These practical and noble goals, so typical of a man of the Enlightenment, were of course transposed into a discordant key by the Revolution and the Terror. In any event, they seem little more than a pretext for Mercier's enraptured inventories. As he admitted, 'I've run about so much to do the *Picture of Paris* that I can say I've done it with *my legs*; and I've learned to walk the pavements of the capital in a manner that is nimble, lively and eager. That's the secret you must possess in order to see everything.' As an observant *flâneur*, he studied the habits of the city's thirty thousand prostitutes, its multitudinous beggars and the six thousand children abandoned every year, its soldiers and police ('They all seem suited to subjugate for ever the outbreak of any serious uprising', Mercier commented with a singular lack of prescience); its washerwomen and greengrocers – as well as that ubiquitous figure, the *décrotteur*, who scraped boots clean after a tromp through the muddy, filthy streets ('He readies you to put in an appearance at the houses of ladies and gentlemen; for you can get away with a slightly worn jacket, a cheap shirt or clothes that have been taken in, but you mustn't arrive with dirty boots, not even if you're a poet').

Like a true *flâneur*, Mercier found his 'research', disorganized and fragmented as it might be, endlessly absorbing. As he put it, 'I haven't been bored once since I started writing books. If I've bored my readers, may they forgive me, since I myself have been hugely amused.'

In the nineteenth century the consummate Parisian *flâneur* was Baudelaire. One of the key texts of the modern urban experience is 'The Painter of Modern Life', in which Baudelaire talks about the caricaturist Constantin Guys (a man who so shunned public attention that Baudelaire refers to him only under the misleading initials M.G.). In one sweeping passage, translated below, Baudelaire extols the modern artist who immerses himself in the bath of the crowd, gathers impressions and jots them down only when he returns to his studio. For him a foray into the cityscape is always undirected, even purposeless – a passive surrender to the aleatory flux of the innumerable and surprising streets.

Of the *flâneur*, Baudelaire writes:

The crowd is his domain, as the air is that of the bird or the sea of the fish. His passion and creed is *to wed the crowd*. For the perfect *flâneur*, for the passionate observer, it's an immense pleasure to take up residence in multiplicity, in whatever is seething, moving, evanescent and infinite: you're not at home, but you feel at home everywhere; you see everyone, you're at the centre of everything yet you remain hidden from everybody – these are just a few of the minor pleasures of those independent, passionate, impartial minds whom language can only awkwardly define. The observer is a prince who, wearing a disguise, takes pleasure everywhere . . . The amateur of life enters into the crowd as into an immense reservoir of electricity.

Baudelaire goes on to compare the *flâneur* to a mirror as huge as the crowd – or to a kaleidoscope outfitted with a consciousness that at every shake of the tube copies the configuration of multifarious life and the graceful movement of all its elements.

Of course we must bear in mind that the cosy, dirty, mysterious Paris Baudelaire is discussing (or Balzac or even the Flaubert of *A Sentimental Education*) is the city that was destroyed after 1853 by one of the most massive urban renewal plans known to history, and replaced by a city of broad, strictly linear streets, unbroken façades, roundabouts radiating avenues, uniform city lighting, uniform street furniture, a complex, modern sewer system and public transportation (horse-drawn omnibuses eventually replaced by the métro and motor-powered buses).

Many people felt that this urban renewal had destroyed the soul of the city. In a play, *Maison neuve*, written by Victorien Sardou in 1866, an older character explains to his niece what he dislikes about the new Paris:

Dear child! It is the old Paris that is lost, the real Paris! A city which was narrow, unhealthy, insufficient, but picturesque, varied, charming, full of memories. We had our favourite walks a step or two away, and our favourite sights, all happily grouped together! We had our little outings with our own folk: how nice it was! . . . Going for a stroll was not something that tired you out, it was a delight. It gave birth to that eminently Parisian compromise between laziness and activity known as *flânerie*! Nowadays, for the least excursions, there are miles to go! . . . An eternal sidewalk going on and on forever! A tree, a bench, a kiosk! . . . A tree, a bench, a kiosk! . . . A tree, a bench . . . This is not Athens any longer, it is Babylon! It is not the capital of France, but of Europe!

Even rebuilt and outfitted with all those identical trees (mostly plane trees and chestnuts), benches and kiosks, more than any other city Paris is still constructed to tempt someone out for an aimless saunter, to walk on just another hundred yards – and then another. Although the métro is the fastest, most efficient and silent one in the world, with stops that are never more than five minutes' walk from any destination, the visitor finds himself lured on by the steeple looming over the next block of houses, by the toy shop on the next corner, the row of antique stores, the shady little square.

August Strindberg, the nineteenth-century Swedish playwright, wandered the Paris streets half-mad and entirely hungry, constantly hallucinating as he read all the flotsam and jetsam of the cityscape as signs and portents. As he records in the short novel-diary *Inferno*, he interpreted everything he saw as messengers from another world (which shows up in his experimental drama *A Dream Play*). High on absinthe, he wandered the city paranoid. He saw the projecting parts of the drum above the Invalides as Napoleon and his marshals, he felt the ground along the Avenue de l'Opéra trembling and on the pavement he found scraps of paper on which someone had written the words *Vulture* and *Marten* (which he took as clear references to his enemy Popoffsky and his wife, who resembled those two animals). The city, which has grown so large it is incomprehensible, can suddenly be deciphered by the seer-drunk-genius in search of little miracles.

The *flâneur* is by definition endowed with enormous leisure, someone who can take off a morning or afternoon for undirected ambling, since a specific goal or a close rationing of time is antithetical to the true spirit of the *flâneur*. An excess of the work ethic (or a driving desire to see everything and meet everyone of recognized value) inhibits the browsing, cruising ambition to 'wed the crowd'.

Americans are particularly ill-suited to be *flâneurs*. They're good at following books outlining architectural tours of Montparnasse or at visiting scenic spots outside Paris – the Désert de Retz, which is a weird collection of follies, for instance, or Rousseau's gardens of Ermenonville, where he meditated in a temple built to resemble a Roman ruin. But they are always driven by the urge towards self-improvement. Typically, Emerson's friend the American thinker and historian Margaret Fuller wrote to him in November 1846 that she had just two weeks in Paris but that she had already attended lectures at the French Academy, visited all the picture galleries and the Chamber of Deputies, met George Sand, heard a short concert by Madame Sand's tubercular lover Chopin and met Poland's leading poet and revolutionary, Adam Mickiewicz, who had advised her to frequent 'the society of Italians' in order to get over her feelings of being ugly (she followed his advice and married a much younger Italian aristocrat). Despite all this activity, she complains to Emerson that she knows she has scanted Paris and 'touched only the glass over the picture'.

At the turn of the nineteenth century the scientific
flâneur (a contradiction in terms, since *flânerie* is
supposed to be purposeless) was Eugène Atget,
an obsessed photographer who was determined
to document every corner of Paris before it disappeared under the assault of modern 'improve-
ments'. He had been born in 1857 near Bordeaux
and as a young man had worked variously as a
sailor, actor and painter. Penniless but driven,
Atget carried his tripod, view camera and glass
plates everywhere with him, shooting all the
monuments but also the fading advertisements
painted on a wall, the dolls in a shop window, the
rain-slick cobbled street, the door knocker, the
quay, the stairwell, even the grain of the wood
steps. He photographed the grand salon of the
Austrian embassy but also street vendors hawk-
ing baskets and the humble horse-drawn fiacre
waiting for a customer. He wore his voluminous
cape everywhere, carrying his heavy equipment
in hands that had been badly scarred by devel-
oping solutions. And he travelled beyond Paris,
too, all the way out to the empty, eerie gardens of
Versailles and the grounds of St Cloud – the
palace northwest of Paris that the communards
had burned down in 1870. Despite his irre-
proachable credentials as a documentalist, Atget
came most into his own when photographing

these pale gods and goddesses in marble, lining the unvisited *allées* of bare winter trees. He would have liked the Christo-wrapped look of the Versailles gardens now; all the statues are covered with protective cloth between All Saints' Day and Easter, and only a hand or toe protrudes.

Atget lived in a tiny studio on the fifth floor of 17 *bis* rue Campagne Première, just off the Boulevard Montparnasse. There he stored his immense collection of *documents pour artistes*, as he called them, and indeed he sold his photos to theatrical decorators, film directors, painters, tapestry makers – anyone who needed a visual record of a vanished Paris. When Berenice Abbott, the young American photographer who virtually discovered him, asked Atget if the French appreciated his work, he said, 'No, only young foreigners.' André Calmette, Atget's oldest friend, told Miss Abbott just after Atget's death:

For twenty years he had lived on milk, bread and bits of sugar. Nobody, nothing, could convince him that these were not the only useful nourishment; all other food was dangerous poison to him. In art and in hygiene he was absolute. He had very personal ideas on everything which he imposed with extraordinary violence. He applied

this intransigence of taste, of vision, of methods,
to the art of photography and miracles resulted.

In the 1920s the founder of Surrealism, André
Breton, turned *flânerie* into a pedantic pathology.
In his novella *Nadja* he pursues a woman
through Paris and accurately records (in words
and photos) each 'sighting', for, as he explains
elsewhere with characteristic fussiness, 'Only the
precise reference, absolutely conscientious, to the
emotional state of the subject at the very moment
in which such events took place can provide a
real basis for appreciation.' Thus the Tour St
Jacques (all that's left of a medieval church that
was demolished by the Revolution in 1797) behind its 'veil' of scaffolding, erected for repairs,
suddenly strikes Breton as 'the world's great
monument to the sphere of the Unrevealed'.
He compares it to a giant sunflower. This ruin
(as well as many buildings, especially the strange
Musée des Arts et Métiers) struck the Surrealists
as essential elements in a 'modern mythology'. As
the German essayist Walter Benjamin remarked,
the Surrealists were attracted to everything that
was out of date, especially 'the first constructions
in steel, the first factories, the oldest photos,
objects that had started to die, living-room pia-
nos, clothes more than five or six years old,

fashionable places that had begun to lose their lustre'.

But the city offers the *flâneur* not only buildings and towers but also amorous adventure. Picasso met one of his mistresses by following the advice of the Surrealists – to cruise the boulevards near the opera house, the Palais Garnier, and befriend the first woman who took his eye. In that way he met his second wife Fernande. The method was no doubt aided by the fact that the French – men and women – like to flirt with strangers in public. Whereas the word *cruise* is part of only the gay vocabulary in English, its French equivalent, *draguer*, is also heterosexual. Straight people cruise one another in Paris; unlike Americans, who feel menaced or insulted by lingering looks on the street, French women – and men! – consider *la séduction* to be one of the arts of living and an amorous glance their natural due. When I lived for several months in the States with a young French man and woman, they were puzzled and hurt at the end of their first American week by the lack of attention they were receiving. 'Maybe Americans don't like our looks?' they asked.

I had to explain to them that American-style feminism had retrained men not to ogle women – but that, more significantly, Americans consider the sidewalk an anonymous backstage space, whereas for the French it is the stage itself. An American office worker on the way to work will not worry about her appearance; she'll change out of her gym shoes into her heels only when she enters her office, whereas a French woman will feel that the instant she hits the streets she's onstage. Clothes, hair and make-up must be impeccable. The French are sometimes excessively concerned about the impression they're making; a mother will spend half an hour picking lint off her daughter's navy-blue suit before they leave the house to set off for Mass. Or a mother will hiss at her little boy in the train, 'Don't speak so loudly, you're drawing attention to yourself.' I asked a French couple who recently visited me in New York for their first impressions after just twenty-four hours in America. The wife said, 'In New York you can tell by people's body language that no one cares what other people think of them, whereas in Paris everyone is judging everyone and the only people who have this American-style insouciance are the insane.'

The last of the great literary *flâneurs* was Walter Benjamin. In a 1929 essay he wrote:

The *flâneur* is the creation of Paris. The wonder is that it was not Rome. But perhaps in Rome even dreaming is forced to move along streets that are too well-paved. And isn't the city too full of temples, enclosed squares, and national shrines to be able to enter undivided into the dreams of the passer-by, along with every paving stone, every shop sign, every flight of steps, and every gateway? The great reminiscences, the historical *frissons* – these are all so much junk to the *flâneur*, who is happy to leave them to the tourist. And he would be happy to trade all his knowledge of artists' quarters, birthplaces, and princely palaces for the scent of a single weathered threshold or the touch of a single tile – that which any old dog carries away. And much may have to do with the Roman character. For it is not the foreigners but they themselves, the Parisians, who made Paris into the Promised Land of *flâneurs*, into 'a landscape made of living people', as Hofmannsthal once called it. Landscape – this is what the city becomes for the *flâneur*. Or, more precisely, the city splits into its dialectical poles. It becomes a landscape that opens up to him and a parlour that encloses him.

In a single packed paragraph Benjamin pinpoints the exact nature of the *flâneur*. He (or she) is not a foreign tourist eagerly tracing down the Major Sights and ticking them off a list of standard wonders. He (or she) is a Parisian in search of a private moment, not a lesson, and whereas wonders can lead to edification, they are not likely to give the viewer gooseflesh. No, it is the private Proustian touchstone – the madeleine, the tilting paving stone – that the *flâneur* is tracking down (not coincidentally, Benjamin was the German translator of the first several volumes of Proust's masterpiece). The weathered threshold, the old tile . . .

In any event, as Benjamin explains, the *flâneur* is in search of experience, not knowledge. Most experience ends up interpreted as – and replaced by – knowledge, but for the *flâneur* the experience remains somehow pure, useless, raw. Practical Romans, who are only annoyed when archaeologists tear up the street yet again to unearth another ugly Etruscan temple, show no curiosity about their city's past, which exists in an all too great abundance. Parisians are the ones who wander their own city.

Walter Benjamin, speaking impersonally but probably referring to himself, recalls several aspects of the *flâneur*. For one thing, he or she is indecisive, unsure of where to go, embarrassed by the richness of his or her choices. As Benjamin puts it, 'Just as waiting seems to be the true state of the motionless contemplative, so doubt seems to be that of the *flâneur*.' Frequently the *flâneur* is tired, having forgotten to eat despite the myriad cafés inviting him or her to come in, relax and partake of a drink or a snack: 'Like an ascetic animal he roams through unknown neighbourhoods until he collapses, totally exhausted, in the foreign, cold room that awaits him.'

In my first years in Paris I felt a shyness about going into cafés where I wasn't known – a timidity peculiar, admittedly, in a man already in his forties. I preferred to wander the streets in the constant drizzle (London has the bad reputation, but Paris weather is not much better). The whole city, at least *intra muros*, can be walked from one end to the other in a single evening. Perhaps its superficial uniformity – the broad avenues, the endlessly repeating benches and lamps stamped from the identical mould, the unvarying metal grates ringing the bases of the trees – promotes the dreamlike insubstantiality of Paris and contributes to the impression of a landscape 'stripped of thresholds'. Without barriers, I found myself gliding along from one area to another. (This inside/outside dichotomy of Paris as experienced by the *flâneur* keeps showing up in Benjamin's notes: 'Just as "*flân-*

erie" can make an interior of Paris, an apartment in which the neighbourhoods are the rooms, so neatly marked off as if with thresholds, in an opposite way the city can present itself to the stroller from all sides as a landscape stripped of all thresholds.')

Eventually I was able to distinguish what Parisians had labelled a 'stuffy' *quartier* from a 'happening' one, a workers' neighbourhood from the home of the young and up-and-coming, but these distinctions were all acquired later and in conversation. At first, when I had to depend on my own observations, Paris impressed me as a seamless unity in which, by American standards, everything was well tended, built to last and at once cold (the pale stone walls, the absence of neon, the unbroken façades never permitted by city ordinance to pass a certain height or to crack or crumble without undergoing a periodic face-lift) *and* discreetly charming (lace curtains in the concierge's window, the flow of cleansing water in the gutters sandbagged to go in one direction or the other, the street fairs with rides for kids, the open-air food markets two days out of every week, segregated into different stalls under low awnings: this one loaded down with spices, that one with jellies and preserved fruits, not to mention the stands of the *pâtissier* and the baker, florist, butcher, fishmonger, the counter selling hot sausages and *choucroute* – or two hundred kinds of cheese). That water in the sandbagged gutter reminds me of something the great American poet John Ashbery once said in discussing the peculiar unaccountability of artistic influence: 'I found my poetry being more "influenced" by the sight of clear water flowing in the street gutters, where it is (or was) diverted or dammed by burlap sandbags moved about by workmen, than it was by the French poetry I was learning to read at the time.'

Imagine dying and being grateful you'd gone to heaven, until one day (or one century) it dawned on you that your main mood was melancholy, although you were constantly convinced that happiness lay just around the next corner. That's something like living in Paris for years, even decades. It's a mild hell so comfortable that it resembles heaven. The French have such an attractive civilization, dedicated to calm pleasures and general tolerance, and their taste in every domain is so sharp, so sure, that the foreigner (especially someone from chaotic, confused America) is quickly seduced into believing that if he can only become a Parisian he will at last master the art of living. Paris intimidates its visitors when it doesn't infuriate them, but be-

The Flâneur

hind both sentiments dwells a sneaking suspicion that maybe the French have got it right, that they have located the *juste milieu*, and that their particular blend of artistic modishness and cultural conservatism, of welfare-statism and intense individualism, of clear-eyed realism and sappy romanticism – that these proportions are wise, time-tested and as indisputable as they are subtle.

If so, then why is the *flâneur* so lonely? So sad? Why is there such an elegiac feeling hanging over this city with the gilded cupola gleaming above the Emperor's Tomb and the foaming, wild horses prancing out of a sea of verdigris on the roof of the Grand Palais? This city with the geometric tidiness of its glass pyramid, Arch of Triumph and the chilly portal imprinted by the Grande Arche on a cloudy sky? Why is he unhappy, this foreign *flâneur*, even when he strolls past the barnacled towers of Nôtre-Dame soaring above the Seine and a steep wall so dense with ivy it looks like the side of a galleon sinking under moss-laden chains?

CHAPTER TWO

PERHAPS THE *FLÂNEUR* should turn away from matronly, pearl-grey Paris, the city built by Napoleon III and his henchman Baron Haussmann, and inhabited today by foreign millionaires, five-star hotels, three-star restaurants and embassies: a phantom city. For the real vitality of Paris today lies elsewhere – in Belleville and Barbès, the teeming *quartiers* where Arabs and Asians and blacks live and blend their respective cultures into new hybrids. This book is dedicated to the random wanderings of the *flâneur*, but his wanderings will take him more often to the strange corners of Paris than to its historic centre, to the strongholds of multiculturalism rather than to the classic headquarters of the Gallic tradition.

Not long ago I was invited to one of those *mondain* dinners the French know how to give with such grace, and that are made up of such startling combinations of guests that they are invariably exciting and (to use a favourite French word that always makes Americans bridle) terribly 'amusing'. A famous historian was there with his wife, as were Pierre Soulages, the painter, and his wife as well as the dress designer Azzadine Alaia and his partner. The host was Jean-Jacques Aillagon, the director of the Centre Georges Pompidou. We were all talking about how Paris was changing. I piped up and said, 'First of all, the average Parisian is no longer white.' Everyone looked shocked and dismayed. Then they all laughed ruefully. I was surprised by their surprise. Wasn't it perfectly obvious that Paris was now a black and tan (and golden yellow) town? Perhaps until that moment they had never thought about the true change in the complexion of their capital.

One person who eagerly embraces the shift in the Parisian colour spectrum is the Spanish novelist Juan Goytisolo. He has lived in the Sentier, the garment district, since the early 1960s. As a leftist – and later as someone who announced his homosexuality loud and clear – Goytisolo had chosen to become an exile from Franco's Spain. One day in Paris he discovered that all the graffiti on his neighbourhood walls were written in

Turkish or Arabic; he decided he should get busy learning the languages of his neighbours. At the same time he was discovering the importance of Arabic and Hebrew in the formation of his own native Spanish culture under Moorish rule.

In a recent essay, 'Paris, Capital of the Twenty-first Century?', Goytisolo wrote of 'the slow de-Europeanization of the capital – the appearance of souks and Turkish baths, strolling salesmen of totems and necklaces, graffiti in Turkish and Arabic', and he observes that this heterogeneity 'extends an invitation to versatile *flânerie* in which a mysterious lesson in the city's layout is woven and torn up, like Penelope's web'. He goes on to assert that the only way France can continue to function as a beacon of civilization, as anything more than a custodian of its great heritage, is by embracing the international, hybridized culture that is already thriving within the city limits. In so doing, Goytisolo dismisses the Paris of grandiose monuments and of 'calm neighbourhoods for tourists, for the retired and for war widows', and defends the Paris of cultural and ethnic cohabitation.

Perhaps the most easily assimilated foreigners in Paris, at least during this century, have been South Americans. They have often been political exiles, fleeing from a dictator, and their plight has been one calculated to appeal to French sympathies. And then their own culture (and language) have oriented them from the very beginning to Paris.

Buenos Aires, with its broad avenues and Beaux-Arts public buildings, was designed to resemble Paris. In the 1960s, when Peron was in power and Spain was still in the grip of Franco, Argentinian artists and intellectuals fled Buenos Aires not for Madrid but for Paris. Hector Bianciotti, one of the best novelists in France today, made his way first to Italy (whence his grandparents had emigrated for Argentina) and eventually to Paris, where he arrived young and penniless. He was soon taken in hand by Leonor Fini, a Surrealist painter who had been born in South America and raised in that most international of all cities, Trieste, before settling in Paris. She introduced him to *le Tout-Paris*. For years he wrote his novels in Spanish, while turning out lots of literary journalism in French (what the French call *un travail alimentaire*, work to buy food), but finally in the 1990s he took the plunge and switched to French – a French, moreover, so polished and refined that soon enough he was made a member of the French Academy itself!

Alfredo Arias is another Argentinian who has become prominent. With a handful of French-speaking Argentine actors (some of them with quite heavy accents) he founded the Théâtre TSE in the 1960s and over the years he has put on many outstanding productions. He collaborated with Juan Piñero, a diminutive Argentine playwright and novelist who died of AIDS in the 1980s.

Brazilians have contributed much to the cultural life of Paris – the concert pianist Nelson Freire, the journalist Bernardo Carvalho, the theatre actor Antonin Interlandi and the editor Alexandre Rosa (who started the first internet book review) are just a few names that spring to mind. But there are also all the Brazilian restaurants and clubs and cabarets that lend such sexy, gyrating animation to the city.

When I came to stay with two French friends in May 1981 for a few weeks, I was given the couch in their apartment on the rue de la Goutte d'Or. They were young guys from Brittany in their late twenties (one was on his way to becoming my first translator) and they weren't earning much; my future translator was teaching French in a lycée in a dangerous northern suburb, and his lover was the manager of a public university lunch room. They'd bought a spacious two-bedroom apartment on the top floor of a nineteenth-century building in the heart of the Arab quarter, mainly because it was affordable but also because the location appealed to their progressive politics.

A block away a food market was set up every few days under the elevated tracks of the métro at the Barbès Rochechouart stop. Piles of melons, little mountains of saffron, cinnamon and coriander seeds, tin wells full of various grades of couscous grains – it was a strip of colourful Marrakesh set down in the greyest section of the city. Just below my friends' windows bearded old men in lace caps were selling caftans on the street – and kids were selling drugs. At night I'd stand on the balcony and look down at the buyers and sellers swarming in the darkness, or standing around a bonfire someone had lit and the police were too nervous to question or extinguish.

François Mitterrand had just been elected President of the Republic and people like my friends were ecstatic. I suppose if a leftist president were ever to be elected in the States, American intellectuals would experience a comparable high – all the more exalting back then, before Mitterrand had actually served for his two compromised, corrupt terms of fourteen years, and before the Eastern bloc of Communist countries had split up and even die-hards had to acknowledge that a state-directed command economy never works. In those happy, optimistic days, however, young people, artists and intellectuals were dancing in the streets. Gays and feminists and Arab and black leaders were all especially delighted, since the man whom they'd campaigned for had won – and now owed them something.

The translator and his lover had the philosopher Michel Foucault, whom I'd met back in New York, to dinner – and only years later, when I was doing research for my biography of Jean Genet and Foucault was already dead, did I realize that in the early 1970s the two men, Genet and Foucault, had campaigned together for the rights of prisoners and Arab immigrants, and a stormy demonstration had brought them both to the rue de la Goutte d'Or. On 27 October 1971, a sixteen-year-old Algerian named Djilali had been killed – shot by a certain Daniel Pigot, who claimed that Djilali had attempted to rape Madame Pigot. Monsieur Pigot had been given a mere seven-month sentence, and some four thousand people demonstrated in the Arab quarter of the rue de la Goutte d'Or: among them Foucault and Genet.

If the rue de la Goutte d'Or is the Paris centre of the trashy, scary Arab scene (or *was*, since it's recently been cleaned up so much it's been virtually expunged), then one of the high, serious

places of traditional Arab culture is the Institut
du Monde Arabe – a sleek, curving glass building
along the Seine, on the Left Bank, looking out at
the Île St Louis. The Institute, designed by France's best architect, Jean Nouvel, and opened in
1987, houses temporary exhibitions and a permanent library and hosts countless conferences
and concerts on Arab–French themes. The building is an innovative blend of Muslim and European architecture. The materials are sleek and
contemporary but the rear façade is an adaptation of the *moucharabieh* (in North African
houses the balcony enclosed with latticework,
often used to let women in the harem see without
being seen). Here there are 27,000 aluminium
openings that dilate or contract according to the
brightness of the sunlight – or at least that's the
idea. Most of the time the delicate photographic
cells linked to a computer are on the blink.

I once gave a talk on Jean Genet's involvement
with the Palestinians here, at the very beginning
of the seven years of research I did for my Genet
biography. Then as now I was nervous about
speaking in public in French, but I was particularly apprehensive about addressing an audience
that would include such prominent Palestinians
as the editor of the *Palestinian Review* and Leila
Shahid, the Palestinians' representative in Paris.

Shahid was especially important to me since she
had been with Genet in Beirut in September
1982, when he had witnessed the violence
wreaked on the Palestinian refugee camp of Shatila – and had immediately begun to write his first
real text in twenty years, *Four Hours at Shatila*.
Shahid and Genet had remained friends until his
death (in fact she was one of the main sources of
information about the last four years of his life).

I was convinced that the Palestinians would
detest me as a Christian and an American, but the
speech went unexpectedly well, since they could
see I took Genet's politics seriously and had done
extensive research. Later I realized how foolish
my fears had been; the Palestinians are the intellectual leaders of the Arab world and far too
sophisticated to confuse an individual with his
nationality or religious background.

In Paris the other pole of Arab culture is the
Mosquée de Paris, across the street from the
botanical garden, the Jardin des Plantes. On
one side of the mosque (built in 1926), at the
corner of rue Geoffroy St-Hilaire and the rue
Daubenton, is what might be called the secular
entrance, to the Turkish bath, the souk, the tea-
room and the couscous restaurant. The *hammam*
is open to men on Tuesdays and Sundays and to
women the other days of the week. It is laid out in

the traditional way, with a hot, steamy room, a tepid one, and a charming room-temperature chamber of cots around a tinkling fountain. The masseurs serve hot, sugared mint tea in little painted glasses as one dozes in the filtered glow of stained-glass windows. Although many gay men go to the *hammam* on Sundays (most of them non-Muslims), they understand they are in a house of worship and they look but do not touch – a rule that adds a civilizing distance to their cruising.

The other, main entrance on the rue du Puits de l'Ermite leads into linked patios planted with roses and walkways under green-tiled arcades. The arches are finished off in carved cedarwood and supported by short red columns. Abstract, intricate tilework runs up the walls to waist height. The inner sanctum of this religious half of the mosque is the hall of worship, forbidden to non-Muslims. But every element on both sides of this complex of buildings breathes calm and spirituality, even the walled tea garden where visitors eat baklava and sip mint tea and sparrows beg for crumbs.

Paris has been at the centre of the myth about racial equality since the time of the Revolution. On the continent of Europe itself slavery had disappeared by the sixteenth century, but it continued to exist in colonies in the West Indies, South America and Africa, and the French sold slaves to the American colonies. In 1788 the French Society of the Friends of Blacks (La Société des Amis des Noirs) was founded; it numbered among its members the philosopher Condorcet, the political leader Mirabeau and the French hero of the American Revolution, Lafayette. The Abbé Raynal was the leading champion of abolition during the Enlightenment.

By 1792 equal rights had been declared for free blacks and in 1794 slavery had been abolished altogether, at home and in the colonies – but Napoleon re-established it in 1802. Slave-trading was not outlawed again in France until 1815 and slavery itself was not definitively abolished in French colonies until 1848. The Revolution had, however, at least established the principle of human equality and abrogated all hereditary privilege. These ideals continued to haunt the political imagination for generations – and still do today.

In the nineteenth century a few black Americans, especially from French-speaking Louisiana, lived and worked in France as actors, painters and writers. The playwright Victor Séjour, from New Orleans, was celebrated in Paris.

At the national school of painting and sculpture, the École des Beaux-Arts, the New Orleans-born Julian Hudson studied in the 1830s, as did the painter Jules Lion. And Charles Ethan Porter, a black American painter armed with a letter of introduction from Mark Twain, was enrolled there from 1881 to 1884. Julian Francis Abele, who later designed the Free Library in Philadelphia, studied architecture at the Beaux-Arts from 1901 to 1905.

Yet until the twentieth century so few French people had seen blacks, especially in the countryside, that the peasants gawked when regiments of black American soldiers ('stevedores', or workers in uniform) – some two hundred thousand strong – arrived in France towards the end of the First World War. Black Americans in uniform were not allowed to fight, only to perform such menial jobs as burying the hundreds of thousands of Allied dead. In order to see combat as soldiers, one black American battalion was forced to sign up with the French army, and they became the famous Harlem Hellfighters, who wore American uniforms but carried French weapons. A secret memo from General Pershing to his French counterparts forbade fraternization between black Americans and white French soldiers; the two nations were expressly forbidden even to shake hands across racial lines. Apparently, back in the States, Southern racists were particularly worried that contact with the French would give 'their' Negroes 'uppity' ideas.

Their fears were justified. Although many French peasants were frightened by their appearance and their reputation as savages, the American blacks' dignity and politeness instantly reassured them. Soon the success of black American soldiers with French women infuriated the white Americans, and white racist antagonism against their own countrymen puzzled the French. White American soldiers would get into fistfights with black soldiers whenever they saw them dancing or embracing French prostitutes in Montmartre. Amid all the clamour and controversy, one prostitute is reported to have shouted at the white Americans, 'This is disgusting! This is France, not Chicago.'

As Tyler Stovall, a black American brought up in Paris, writes in his recent *Paris Noir: African Americans in the City of Light*:

Although the myth of French colour blindness already existed among black Americans, the experiences of their soldiers in France during World War I powerfully reinforced it. In March 1919, W.E.B. Du Bois published a landmark article,

'The Black Man in the Revolution of 1914–18', in *The Crisis*. Arguing that 'The black soldier saved civilization' during the war years, Du Bois emphasized the kind treatment these men had received from the French. Even after their return to a hostile America, Du Bois noted, 'They will ever love France.' Similarly, a black private wrote home, 'There is an air of liberty, equality and fraternity here which does not blow in the black man's face in liberty-loving, democratic America . . .'

In the years between the wars African American entertainers took Paris by storm. And Montmartre, the centre for seedy nightlife then and now, was their district. In fact, the war wasn't even over yet when jazz was being played for the first time in Paris (a style that almost instantly influenced the French composer Maurice Ravel). Louis Mitchell performed in Paris in November 1917 with his group the Seven Spades, and the same year a black orchestra, the Jazz Kings, appeared at the Casino de Paris. The casino was at number 16 rue de Clichy, which runs behind the Trinité church up the hill to the Place de Clichy. The 815th Pioneer Infantry band, led by Lieutenant Jimmy Europe, made history when it played in Paris during the Conference of Allied

Women in August 1918. In 1919 Joe Zelli, a restaurateur from London, opened a club that dominated the Montmartre jazz scene until the 1930s. The programming was done by Eugene Bullard, who'd been born in Mississippi in 1894 and who'd grown up being told by his father that 'in France there are not different white churches and black churches, or white schools and black schools, or white graveyards and black graveyards'. As American blacks quickly discovered, the French could be prejudiced, but their basic attitude seemed to be live and let live, and racism had never been *institutionalized* in modern France, never confirmed and upheld by law.

Bullard had stowed away on a ship when he was just ten years old and made his way first to Berlin, then to London, and finally to Paris in 1913. When the war broke out he joined the French Foreign Legion and won the Croix de Guerre at Verdun. He ended up in the Lafayette Flying Corps, a volunteer group of American pilots who fought for France before America entered the war. When the Americans at last joined the fray in 1917, Bullard was transferred to the American air force – and instantly grounded because of his colour.

By the mid-1920s there were scores of black Montmartre hangouts – notably Bricktop's. Ada

Louise Smith, known as Bricktop because of her red hair, had been born in Chicago in the 1890s and arrived in Paris in 1924. As a singer back in Harlem, Bricktop had picked up the knack of joking with and performing for an elite white audience at the aptly named Exclusive Club. Eugene Bullard, who in 1924 was managing a club called Le Grand Duc in Montmartre, heard about her and invited her to sing for his chic clientele. When Bricktop saw how tiny the Paris venue was, just a dozen tables and a dance floor, she burst into tears, but soon she was belting out songs to, among others, F. Scott Fitzgerald. 'My greatest claim to fame,' Fitzgerald declared, 'is that I discovered Bricktop before Cole Porter did.' She often regaled her audience with Cole's sombre-witty 'Miss Otis Regrets'. She also entertained the humorous writer Anita Loos (*Gentlemen Prefer Blondes*), the photographer Man Ray and his muse and mistress Kiki – a model and painter from Burgundy and the self-declared queen of Montmartre. The American novelist Kay Boyle remembered years later that Bricktop was a woman to be cherished: 'I liked her tinted brick-coloured hair, her cocoa flesh, her lively and almost impossibly beautiful legs, her dogwood white teeth, her clear-eyed poise in the dancing, drinking, worldly turmoil of the place

. . . The decisions she took in the hour we spent with her that night were made as quietly as the turning of the pages of a book . . .'

The dishwasher in the kitchen was a youngster who would turn out to be the great Harlem Renaissance poet Langston Hughes. While working at Bricktop's he wrote his verses 'Jazz Band in a Parisian Cabaret', which he sold to *Vanity Fair*. In another poem, he wrote:

> Soft light on the tables,
> Music gay,
> Brown-skin dancers
> in a cabaret.

Eventually Bricktop opened her own club nearly across the street, financed by the couturier Elsa Schiaparelli. Here Mabel Mercer – who was singing on a record at the first gay cocktail party I ever attended in Ann Arbor, Michigan, in the 1950s – performed her 'sophisticated' repertoire of naughty or world-weary songs (her signature song was 'Bye Bye Blackbird'). Gossip used to have it that Mercer and Bricktop were lovers. Mabel Mercer had such a snooty British accent and such rolling **r**'s that no one would ever have confused her with a New Orleans blues singer (Frank Sinatra later claimed he learned every-

thing he knew about vocal phrasing from her).
Today Bobby Short is her direct artistic heir.

Bricktop could always be persuaded at some
point in the evening to sing her favourite tune,
'Insufficient Sweetie'. The Prince of Wales (later
King Edward VIII and, after his abdication, the
Duke of Windsor) was a friend; he was such a
party boy – and such a devotee of *le jazz hot* –
that once, attending a show in London, he had
the curtains closed around the royal box so that
he could Charleston alone in peace, unobserved
by his subjects. Capricious and slightly idiotic, he
once made a band play Noël Coward's 'A Room
with a View' nine times in a row.

After I moved to Paris in 1983 I kept getting into
conversations with friendly French people who
would bring up the name of Sidney Bechet to
show me how much they knew about American
culture. I think I shocked them when I revealed I
had no idea who Bechet was. Only later did I
discover that this gifted African American musician, a master of the clarinet and especially the
soprano saxophone, and perhaps the first great
jazz soloist on any instrument, had spent the last
third of his life in France and become rich and
famous there – but only there. Born in New
Orleans in 1897, Bechet had started off as a

Edmund White

clarinettist when he was just fifteen years old with a group called the Eagle Band. He teamed up soon enough with a young cornet player called Louis Armstrong.

In 1919 Bechet was in London with the Southern Syncopated Orchestra, where for the first time he was working in concert halls, not in obscure clubs as in New York or Chicago. In England he even had the honour of being singled out in a review by Ernest Ansermet, the Swiss conductor of the Orchestre de la Suisse Romande, who wrote one of the first serious analyses of jazz ever published (and which Bechet had translated into English and widely reprinted). Ansermet spoke of Bechet's 'perfectly formed blues' which he 'elaborated at great length' in riffs 'admirable for their richness of invention, force of accent, and daring in novelty and the unexpected'.

If listeners had anything to complain of, it was Bechet's wide, invariable vibrato, a tic that alienated many potential fans. But everyone, especially his colleagues, had to recognize his fantastic musical memory; he would never agree to learn to read music, fearful that it would make him lose his powers of improvisation – yet he could memorize an entire score just by hearing it played through once or twice, and he picked up not only his own part but everyone else's as well.

Bechet was also known for his hot temper. He liked to brag that he treated his women rough – knocked them around and got rid of them at the least sign of rebellion. He was accused of assaulting a woman in London and was sentenced to fourteen days of hard labour and deportation. A decade later, on 20 December 1928, Bechet got into a gun fight with Mike McKendrick, another jazz musician, at Bricktop's in Paris over a small question of musical interpretation. The two men began firing at each other. Bechet was imprisoned for a year and then ordered to leave the country. Even this misadventure, however, did not convince him to lay aside his weapons, and till the end of his life he packed a pistol wherever he went.

After such an inauspicious beginning, Bechet's subsequent triumphs in France are all the more remarkable. By 1931 he was allowed back in the country on a one-month visa, but he did not make his real mark in France until 1949, when he returned for a festival and discovered that a few assiduous French fans had been following every tiny detail of his career and knew his discography better than he himself did. America may make B movies or *films noirs* and give birth to jazz soloists, but only the French have treated these forms as artistic from the very beginning and applied to them a flattering pedantry. More than once I've had French friends tut-tut and remark that my 'film culture' or my 'jazz connoisseurship' was regrettably not very 'deep' (read: nonexistent).

In Bechet's case, one of his French fans was the band leader and clarinettist Claude Luter (who was twenty-six years old in 1949). The two men began to play dates together in Paris and to record together: the beginning of a very long collaboration.

Soon Bechet was a national French hero. His recordings were played on the radio, his concerts were sold out and hordes of young fans charged the closed doors of theatres wherever he performed. The Existentialists in St-Germain-des-Prés took him up, and so did an ever-growing general public. Bechet knew how to cultivate his success. He played jazz versions of French classics such as 'Mon Homme' (made famous by Mistinguett, the great *chanteuse*) and composed new songs with French titles, 'Les Oignons' and 'Petite Fleur' being the best known. As his biographer John Chilton has written, Bechet 'was creating an Afro-American-Gaulish fare that was unlike anything else being played in the jazz world'. Bechet was convinced that jazz had both

French and African roots, since it had started in the formerly French town of New Orleans. And, as he put it, 'France, it's closer to Africa.'

The public loved him – partly because he had a French last name, partly because he spoke volubly in a mixture of Creole and heavily accented French, but mainly because he was as friendly as he was gifted. Maybe they also liked him because he was mysterious, concealing his true thoughts under a veneer of bonhomie, a man who was by turns fiercely violent and self-assertive and so agreeable in an abstract way that he was sometimes accused of being an Uncle Tom. In short, he was a hard-to-classify individual, which the French always admire. His portrait was printed on a brand of French chocolates, and French instrument makers eagerly sought his endorsements. By 1955 the French review *Le Jazz Hot* was referring to Bechet as 'our own Sidney'. Bechet was deluged with French wines, women and more and more songs. 'By 1956,' writes Chilton, 'Sidney's record sales in France were comparable with those of the leading pop stars.'

A Bechet fan club was organized and held its first meeting on a *bâteau mouche* on the Seine. Every French radio station was regularly playing Bechet recordings. As one American visitor to Paris said: 'Sidney could have become mayor of

Paris if he wanted to. Crowds of people followed him through the streets. I was never so surprised in my whole life as when I discovered that a compatriot, whom I had barely heard of, had become the darling of the French.'

When Bechet died on his sixty-second birthday, on 14 May 1959, he had become the very image of the successful Frenchman. He had a wife *and* a mistress with a child, two mansions – and a funeral *cortège* of some three thousand people. The chic resort town of Juan-les-Pins on the Riviera erected a statue to him, and his memoirs, *Treat it Gentle*, had not only been edited by the American poet John Ciardi but also translated into French by Boris Vian, one of the most popular novelists in Paris and himself an avid jazz fan and performer.

When Josephine Baker had first sailed over to France in 1925, she'd met and been befriended by a fellow passenger, Sidney Bechet, with whom she'd had a shipboard romance and who helped her out during a concert at sea when she forgot the melody for an instant. The nineteen-year-old Baker had already been in show business for five years, most recently in the musical revues *Shuffle Along* and *The Chocolate Dandies*. Raised in St Louis in extreme poverty, she had been a frightened young witness to the appalling St Louis race riots of 1917 in which thirty-nine blacks were killed and thousands left homeless. When she was just eight years old she'd been sent to work for a white woman who plunged her hands in boiling water because she used too much soap in the wash. Her hands were burned so severely that she had to be hospitalized.

Now, in Paris, Josephine was a member of the cast of the Revue Nègre, a song-and-dance troupe put together in New York by the bored wife of an American diplomat stationed in Paris. The organizer realized that such an evening would thrill the Parisians – and indeed no sooner did the show open than French journalists were burbling along happily about 'the triumph of lubricity, a return to the manners of the child-hood of man', or waxing lyrical about 'planta-tion landscapes, the melancholy songs of Creole nurses, the Negro soul with its animal energy, its childish joys, the sad bygone time of slavery . . .' Jean Cocteau, ever alert to a trend, declared that with Josephine, 'Eroticism has found a style.' Erich Maria Remarque, the author of *All Quiet on the Western Front*, 'remarqued' that Baker brought 'a whiff of jungle air and an elemental strength and beauty to the tired showplace of Western Civilization'.

Baker preferred Sidney Bechet's music (played while he was dressed up as a peanut vendor) to anyone else's performance – including her own. And she was both realistic and straightforward about her own appeal: 'The rear end exists. I see no reason to be ashamed of it. It's true there are rear ends so stupid, so pretentious, so insignificant that they're good only for sitting on.' Hers was good for vibrating at humming-bird speed. And just when the French males in the audience began panting audibly over her 'savage' appeal (her number was called 'Danse sauvage'), Josephine would turn around, cross her eyes and give a giddy what-me-worry grin. She was sexual because she had a beautiful body, danced barebreasted and eventually wore a belt of bananas, but her sensuality was light-hearted, speedy, given to clowning – and, as Cocteau had discerned, 'stylish'. In her first two years in Paris she received 46,000 fan letters and some 2,000 marriage proposals.

She had a very high little voice that went with her overbite and her vibrating body – really nothing more than the squeak of a chipmunk on amphetamines. You keep checking to see if the tape is on rapid rewind when you listen to her sing 'J'ai deux Amours' or 'La petite Tonkinoise'. But the one time I saw her on stage in New York, at the very end of her career, after half a century in show business and two years before her death in 1975, she was a wonderfully touching and half-camp monument to herself. She opened her second act after the interval on a motorcycle, but she also treated everyone to tits, ass, feathers and a rhinestone mike as she roamed the audience and sat on the laps of elderly retired Pullman conductors.

She sang 'I Did It My Way', which took on a special poignancy in her case, since in the early seventies she was getting some grief from black political leaders for having left her own country. She might have reminded these critics she could never have had the career in the States that she'd enjoyed in France, for after all she'd reigned supreme in her country of adoption as *the* leading variety artist. When she'd attempted to return to Broadway in the thirties, American audiences had laughed at her baby-doll voice, and hotels had refused to put her up because of her race. In France she'd owned a Renaissance château in the Dordogne, even though she failed to pay for it and was finally evicted. She'd had Marshal Tito offer her an island where she could house the 'rainbow tribe' of children she'd adopted from various national backgrounds. She had an affair with the famous mystery writer Georges Simenon, who claimed her as one of the most memorable of the ten thousand women he'd made love to by the age of eighty. She even had an affair with Bricktop, soon after her arrival in France; at least one of Josephine's adopted sons, Jean-Claude Baker, claimed that he'd had this gossip straight from Bricktop's own mouth.

According to Phyllis Rose's *Jazz Cleopatra*, the French waiters in New York had told Josephine when she was first on her way to Paris that she could seduce their countrymen if she was chic and could make them laugh. Her mugging certainly amused them, and her flair for clothes brought them to their knees. She was dressed by the most famous *couturier* of the day, Paul Poiret. According to one tale, she rejected all his clothes as the models showed them to her; at last, unable to speak French at the time, she laughed and drew the design she wanted: a shimmy dress covered with fringe that was shaded from pink at the top to red at the bottom. The delighted Poiret made it and included it in his next collection.

Josephine did learn French quickly and soon became a fixture of French society. During the war she sided with de Gaulle and entertained his troops and black American soldiers based in Morocco. She was an active member of the Resistance and was made a lieutenant in the Free

French army, and in the 1960s she was awarded the Legion of Honour and the Rosette of the Resistance.

In those postwar years the African American presence in Paris began to include more and more artists, writers and intellectuals and not just performers. The three most distinguished writers were Richard Wright, James Baldwin and Chester Himes, and all three went to a soul-food restaurant, the Haynes Grill at 3 rue Clauzel, in the lower fringe of Montmartre – which still preserves a faint echo of that more exciting era. When a major conference, on African Americans and Europe, was held in Paris in February 1992 at a branch of the Sorbonne, the restaurant played host to many of the participants. And even now, whenever black American artists visit Paris, they're sure to stop by Haynes for a bite. Tyler Stovall declares flatly that the 'Haynes restaurant is the pre-eminent black American institution in Paris today'. Nowadays the second Mrs Haynes – an adept of her late husband's Southern soul-food recipes, a Frenchwoman named Maria – rustles up the collard greens and ham hocks and cornbread, while amateur jazz musicians perform and pass the hat. On the cream-coloured stucco walls are photos of the celebrities who have dined here, including the black actors Ruby Dee and

Ossie Davis and such musicians as the Four Inkspots and Dinah Washington, Louis Armstrong and Lionel Hampton.

The head waiter – some nights the only waiter – is Benny Luke, a tall, handsome California native who, more than twenty years ago, played the part of the black transvestite maid in the original French film version (and stage play) of *La Cage aux Folles*. He's the one who knelt in tears before his transvestite boss and implored in his heavy American accent, '*Maîtresse, Maîtresse!*' The first time I went to the Haynes Grill, Benny looked quite different from his image in the film. He's still svelte but now he's bald and very macho, and he kept us at arm's length by speaking to us in French – a very formal French at that. But at last, since my American friend and I were the only customers, Benny finally broke down and spoke to us in English – after all, we were three Americans, which seemed more important than our skin colour on a rainy February night in Paris. Most of the customers these days are French, however.

Leroy Haynes, who had come originally from Georgia, was in the American army during the Second World War but stayed on in Paris after the armistice. He had been a big burly football player but in Paris he acted – his roles included the lead in *Daddy Goodness,* Richard Wright's 1960 adaptation of Louis Sapin's play *Papa Bon Dieu.* When Wright began a Franco-American fellowship club to promote friendship between the French and the black Americans living in Paris, Leroy Haynes was the first president of the organization. It was not just a sort of Kiwanis Club; it actively opposed racist incidents in the States, including the 'legal lynching' of seven young black men in Virginia who'd been accused on the flimsiest of evidence of raping a white woman. Already Paris was becoming an offshore base and headquarters for some of the most important thoughts and acts concerning the increasingly volatile issue of race in America.

Perhaps an indication of how small the black American population was in Paris is that both James Baldwin and Chester Himes ended up attacking Richard Wright, the pope of American black writers in Paris. Baldwin's oedipal lunge came in the form of an essay against Wright's type of thesis fiction, 'Everybody's Protest Novel', and Himes based a self-righteous, hypocritical character on Wright in the novel *A Case of Rape*.

Wright had left the States for France on 1 May 1946 after a long hassle trying to get a passport – which may or may not have been deliberately delayed because Wright was a well-known critic of American racism and the authorities didn't want his sharp tongue exported. What's undeniable is that shortly before Wright made his final decision to leave the States, he'd been turned down when he wanted to buy a house in New Hampshire. The owner even had the nerve, callousness or sheer ignorant bigotry to tell him that he had decided not to sell to a black man.

Gertrude Stein welcomed the celebrated author of *Black Boy* and *Native Son* to Paris, telling him that he would find France as useful to his writing as she had during the last forty years. She always claimed that she preferred living in a French-speaking world, since it left her alone with English. And Wright optimistically agreed. After checking out her work he said, 'I'd say that one could live and write like that only if one lived in Paris or some out of the way spot where one could claim one's own soul . . .' In any event he was thrilled by what he perceived as the acceptance of all races: 'There is such an absence of race hate that it seems a little unreal.'

Unfortunately, as the years would go by, Wright discovered that his best creative work was behind him and that he was caught up more by the political questions of race than by the exigencies of his art. For one thing, in France he was respected as an intellectual leader, whereas in the States he'd never been accorded this heady status. He was welcomed and his opinion was solicited by Sartre and Camus and Beauvoir; Wright was particularly besotted by Sartre. 'How rare a man is this Sartre,' Wright confided to his journal. 'His ideas must be good because they lead him into areas of life where man sees what is true.'

What fascinated – and sometimes baffled – Wright was the French attitude towards colonialism, and the attitude of the colonized towards France. So successful were the French in convincing black Africans and Caribbeans in their colonies that they were French before all else that any sense of international black solidarity was slow to build up. (Even to this day a visit to Guadeloupe or Martinique will startle an American, for there the islanders are full-fledged French citizens, their countries are *départements* exactly like those in France, the same TV programmes are seen at the same hour, the same curriculum is taught in similar schools, the postal system is the same model of efficiency, as is the generous welfare and unemployment programme. The food is marvellous and the women are chic – even if the food is crab-stuffed chicken leg and the women in home-made Yves Saint-Laurent rip-offs are emerging from tin shacks. For people flying between France and Pointe-à-Pître there is no need to pass through immigration. The Martiniquais and Guadelupeans even have the French right to pay five dollars for a Coke.)

Now, of course, one of the most significant far-right parties in Europe is in France – Le Pen's National Front. And even though it was losing votes near the end of the twentieth century, ten years earlier it had garnered some 15 per cent of the national vote on a platform that included the (illegal) denial of the Holocaust, as well as a policy of 'France for the French'.

If the French are racist, it is primarily against Arabs, whom they euphemistically call North Africans or maghrebins. The loss of Algeria as a colony during the protracted and painful war for independence which began in the late 1950s and ended in 1962 had exacerbated the hostility. Hundreds of thousands of French colonists had been forced to return to France, though in some cases their families had lived and worked in Algeria for more than a hundred years. At roughly the same time a few million Arabs emigrated to France. When the economy began to slide, Le Pen's party exploited the situation with the slogan 'Three million unemployed, three million immigrants'.

In the late 1950s Richard Wright was afraid to denounce de Gaulle's war against the Algerians, for fear of being expelled and repatriated. He had left America in a rage and had been a stalwart defender of France and French tolerance. Now he feared being deported to his hated native land. His expatriation had cost him dear. Whereas a stylist like Gertrude Stein could revel in her solitude with the English language, Wright was out of touch with the rapidly evolving race war in the States – which was his main subject. As a writer he suffered as much as James Jones did – a white American novelist and the author of *From Here to Eternity*, his Second World War novel based on American speech patterns and drawn directly from his battle experience. Although Jones was able to repeat his success in one book he wrote during his many years in Paris, *The Thin Red Line*, otherwise he seemed disoriented and sterile. He never bothered to learn French and hung out mostly with fellow Americans. His buddy, the novelist Irwin Shaw, also stayed encysted among other Americans – and with a similar disastrous effect on his career. As James Dickey, the American poet, wrote contemptuously in 1954 to a friend, 'Paris is a great city for writers; that is, for the kind of writers who need other writers around, who need the "literary life", who need to discuss and drink together . . .'

Wright, Jones and Shaw had all arrived in Paris when they were already highly successful, and the Paris they inhabited was one of luxurious apartments and elegant restaurants. Those American writers who seemed to prosper the most in Paris were the ones who came when they were still young and struggling (William Carlos Williams and Hemingway, for instance), or who plunged into contemporary French literature and literary circles (like John Ashbery, Harry Mathews and, to take an earlier example, Edith Wharton), or who used France as a base for gaining a critical distance on their native land and its problems (James Baldwin leaps to mind).

Baldwin did most of his important writing in France, and during the late sixties and early seventies he was severely criticized for living abroad. He wrote one of the first gay novels of the postwar period, *Giovanni's Room*, in which the two male lovers are both white, one an American, the other a Parisian bartender; in this lyrical book the verbal beauty conceals a despair about being gay and a self-hatred implicit in his exclusion of black characters – and of anyone less than beautiful (Baldwin was intensely sensitive about his looks). Nevertheless the whiteness and foreignness of his characters gave him permission to write one of the first – and most convincing – 'out' novels of the epoch. In his essays (for example 'Equal in Paris' or 'The Discovery of What it Means to be American in Europe'), Baldwin concentrated on his situation as an expatriate – and drew strong literary sustenance from it.

During my years in Paris, from 1983 to 1998, I put together my own album of mental snapshots about race. I remember once being with a preppy black friend from the States, a clothes designer, who was stopped as we came out of the métro by a posse of policemen. From time to time the police check the visas or passports of people supposedly selected at random. I hated being so cynical, but I wanted to spare my friend any further embarrassment (and besides, he didn't understand French), so I just said with great confidence to the transit policemen, 'Don't worry, messieurs, he's with me.' And that did it – they let us pass by with no more fuss, virtually saluting.

Another black American friend saw an ad for an apartment and responded on the phone. He was encouraged to come by and see the apartment. (Landlords like to rent to Americans under the table, since they don't have to declare the money as part of their taxable income, and the

Americans usually go back home after a year or two – no danger of sitting tenants when you're dealing with foreigners.) When the landlady saw my friend was black she muttered that the apartment was already rented. Then, after he'd spoken to her a few minutes more, she exclaimed, 'Oh, you're an *American* black – that's much better.' She ended up renting him the apartment after all. She was afraid of African blacks, perceived as more likely to stay for years, to cook strange-smelling foods and invite successive waves of relatives to stay with them in one room or two.

When I lived on the Île St Louis, someone had rented out the *garage* in the courtyard to an African family. Sometimes there were as many as twenty in that small, damp, unheated room. They were using the toilet off the stairs and filling buckets from the tap in the courtyard. They seemed to have rigged up lights and a space heater by running wires into a neighbouring apartment, but it all looked very primitive and dangerous. It was like a bit of the Ivory Coast in our stately, silent town house. Perhaps someone was gouging these poor people for a rent for illegal housing, but the ironic – and completely modern Parisian – side was that the children were attending the local school and no neighbourhood could have been safer. This tranquillity compared favourably with the housing projects outside Paris, which are in neighbourhoods so dangerous that the police refuse to go into them – and where high-school teachers fear for their lives.

Last snapshot: a gym in the fifth arrondissement was offering free three-month memberships in order to encourage new people to join, but when a black American friend presented himself he was told that there were no further vacancies – which led to an ugly scene when a group of us descended on the gym to complain and were hustled out, shouting and protesting. And yet . . .

And yet most of the African Americans surveyed recently still felt that France was less racist than their own country – and, one might add, French racism is more naive and transparent when it does occur (a mixed and backhanded sort of advantage). In a country where a premium is placed on all that is *chic*, right now blacks are chic.

When I asked the doorman of a smart club not long ago what were his criteria for admitting or refusing people, he said, 'Well, first of all we accept all blacks, then all models, then all celebrities . . .'

CHAPTER THREE

THE *FLÂNEUR* WANDERS through the Jewish ghetto in the Marais in the fourth arrondissement. Here, not far from the Hôtel de Ville in a small rectangle – bounded by the rue Vieille du Temple on the west and the rue Pavée on the east, and by the rue des Francs Bourgeois on the north and the rue du Roi de Sicile on the south – are shops selling the Torah and the Hanukkah candelabra, kosher delicatessens, the remains of an old ritual bath and two synagogues. One of them is the Synagogue Fleishman, tiny and hard to find on the rue des Écouffes, and the other is elegant and easier to spot: the Synagogue de la rue Pavée. It was built by recently arrived Polish Jews between 1910 and 1913 and conceived by Hector Guimard, the flamboyant architect who designed the stylish and distinctive *Art Nouveau* entrances to the métro.

Perhaps the best-known landmark in this neighbourhood now is Jo Goldenberg's deli and restaurant. Here, on 9 August 1982, a terrorist bomb killed six people, wounded twenty-two and blew up part of the establishment. Today these memories are virtually forgotten by visitors to the restaurant in the swirl of good food, Gypsy and klezmer music, lively talk and general animation. The walls are hung from chair level to ceiling with sketches of rabbis in prayer shawls and School of Chagall paintings of village fiddlers. It's the one place in Paris where one can strike up a conversation easily with the people at the next table.

The neighbourhood is a gathering place for eastern European Jews, with their poppy-seed cakes and strudels, as well as North African Jews, with their gooey baklavas and charred falafel. Here can be seen Hassidim in long black coats, beards and hats, standing on street corners with their hands behind their backs, discussing theology with one another. And here American Jewish tourists, fatigued with the foreignness of France, are relieved to realize that the well-posted French word *cacher* means 'kosher'. On a warm day, or on any Saturday fair or dismal, the three-block-long rue des Rosiers is so crowded with *flâneurs* that cars can barely push their way through.

Some of the visitors have come to sample the picturesque patisseries, but others are just window-shopping outside the chic new dress stores that have invaded this very old *quartier*. The neighbourhood is so popular that apartment rents are soaring.

The prosperity and sunny look of the ghetto today were not always so in evidence. Until recently this was the quarter of very poor Jews. As Cynthia Ozick has pointed out, one form that anti-Semitism takes is to speak of Jews as if they are and always were rich, whereas in fact most Jews in France (and in Paris) were dreadfully poor. These poor Jews from Russia and Poland, from Alsace and later from Algeria, came to the rue des Rosiers in the nineteenth and twentieth centuries because here they could find cheap rents, a welcoming community and jobs – or news about jobs – as furriers, dressmakers, leather toolers and travelling tinkers. Here they could speak Yiddish (for very few of them spoke French at first), could worship in their synagogues, keep kosher and meet familiar faces at local cafés.

In the history of French Jews, the Revolution must count as a signal event. Jews had been living in Gaul since ancient Roman times, but in the Christian era their fate had never been easy. The low point occurred in 1306 when Philippe le Bel forbade Jews of any sort to live on French soil, an ethnic cleansing announced as a grotesque ideal by his grandfather, St Louis. Some hundred thousand Jews were driven out of France, which was a much smaller country then. They moved to regions that are incorporated into modern France but were then independent – including Provence, Burgundy, Alsace and Lorraine and the Dauphiné (an eastern region that is bordered by the Alps; its capital is Grenoble and it didn't become part of France until 1560). Other expelled Jews went as far as Hungary, Poland, Spain and the Rhine valley.

At the time of the Revolution there were only about 40,000 Jews out of a French population of some 24 million. Half of them lived in Alsace, some 7,000 in Lorraine and about 5,000 in the southwest near Bordeaux. In Paris itself there were only about 500 Jews. No Jew had been granted citizenship, but the Revolutionaries did debate the ideas about Jewish equality that had been advanced by the Enlightenment Jewish philosopher Moses Mendelssohn (grandfather of the composer Felix). In 1789 the Assembly proclaimed in the Declaration of the Rights of Man that all men are born and remain free and equal in their rights – but the document did not take up the status of Jews (nor of slaves in the colonies, nor of women anywhere).

Jews were excluded primarily because they were perceived as a race apart with their own institutions and loyalties, and as outsiders impossible to integrate into the fabric of French society. As the Count de Clermont-Tonnerre, a liberal defender of the Jews, remarked, 'We must refuse everything to Jews as a nation and grant everything to Jews as individuals.' By 1791 Jews in Alsace and Lorraine as well as in newly annexed southern regions were granted citizenship, even if they were invested with full rights only after taking a loyalty oath to the state.

Citizenship under the Revolution and later Napoleon had its drawbacks. Profoundly against religion of all sorts, the Revolutionaries closed synagogues with the same impartiality with which they forbade worship in churches. Assimilation of Jews brought few concrete advantages and threatened the integrity – and isolation – of Jewish communities. Napoleon was hostile to the Jewish population, which had greatly expanded under the Empire and its conquests. He declared in 1806 that

the French government cannot view with indifference a debased, degraded nation capable of all forms of lowness and in the exclusive possession of two fine *départements* of former Alsace; one must think of the Jews as a nation and not as a sect. It constitutes a nation within the nation . . . Entire villages have been expropriated by the Jews; they have replaced feudalism; they are true schools of sharks.

This pseudo-problem of 'nationalism' among Jews has been a persistent theme running throughout European history. The myth is that Jews think themselves better than Christians (as 'the Chosen People') and that they are more loyal to one another than to their 'host' nation. There is a convincing theory that anti-Semitism has been largely replaced in France by anti-Arab sentiment, confirmed by the current French Christian insistence on the supposed Muslim sense of superiority and by a fear of pan-Islamic loyalties.

Responding to Napoleon's charge, the rich Jewish leader from Bordeaux, Abraham Furtado, wrote to the Emperor: 'Israelites in our Temples, French in the midst of our fellow citizens – that's how we are.' But Napoleon wasn't convinced. He was determined to assimilate Jews to the point of extinguishing their separate identity. He ordered Jews to be conscripted into the imperial armies

without the possibility of buying paid replace-
ments (an option open to rich Christians) – and
he commanded a certain percentage of mixed
marriages among Jews and Christians. He also
wanted the Jewish 'nation' under closer scrutiny
and, accordingly, he set up a state-supervised
consistory in every district that counted at least
2,000 Jewish citizens. Each consistory – headed
by rabbis and the local gentry nominated by an
assembly of Jewish notables and confirmed by
the government – was responsible for the welfare
of the local Jewish community and its conformity
to Napoleonic laws. Typical of Napoleon's anti-
Semitism was his insistence that the consistory
encourage Jews to take up 'useful' professions
and not the 'useless' one of lending money,
although the Christian peasants of Alsace-Lor-
raine could get a loan only from their Jewish
neighbours – who were almost all on the same
level of poverty as they but had been traditionally
excluded from owning land and farming. Napoleon's government went so far as to annul most
debts owed to Jews. He also decreed that Jewish
merchants and craftsmen must apply for a licence
every year in order to continue to practise their
trades. All further Jewish immigration into Alsace was forbidden. Finally, Jews were forced to
take up stable family names. Many Jews chose

the names of the towns or cities they were living in.

This drive towards assimilation of the Jews became even more pronounced under the Third Republic, declared in 1871. Starting in 1872, for instance, the French government was forbidden to pose any official questions regarding race or ethnic origins. Resolutely anti-clerical (indeed, opposed to religion of any sort), the Third Republic gave full expression to an old French tradition of secularism. The contemporary French state, by the way, is to a large degree an heir to this tradition. Foreigners, who imagine that France is a Catholic country, are often shocked by the level of fierce anticlericalism that reigns there today.

To illustrate my point about how Muslims have become the Jews of our day, I can mention the case of the *foulard* in the France of the 1990s. Muslim girls who'd been instructed by their religious families to wear to school a head-covering (*not* a veil) and to abstain from gym class, where they'd be forced to expose their bodies to other students and instructors, were suddenly ordered by the Minister of Education to conform to normal school practice. The scarf, or *foulard*, was forbidden, and the girls were obliged to attend exercise classes.

Cultural differences between the French and the Americans were brought out in the open by this hotly debated issue. Whereas the French Republic was created by atheists, the United States, after all, was founded as a refuge for oppressed *religious* groups (Puritans, Quakers, English Catholics, French Huguenots, German Pietists and Lutherans), and America remains, perhaps primarily, a place where cults are free to pursue their separate ideals. As a result Americans (even a fairly Voltairian American like me) are outraged by the notion that a student cannot display a few outward signs of religious allegiance while at school. One can only imagine the outcry in the States if Jewish boys were not permitted to wear their skullcaps or Catholic girls were forbidden the crucifix or other holy medals. When the French are attempting to suss out the States, the one thing they invariably fail to remember is that one out of every three Americans has had a personal conversation with Jesus Christ. The strangely personal character of evangelical Protestantism remains a mystery even to those few French Catholics who are believers and practising (in the French formula, *croyant et pratiquant*).

Despite lingering anti-Semitism, Jews appeared to be winning acceptance in the France of Napoleon III and the Third Republic. One sign of this acceptance was the role Jews were playing at every level of government service: in the post office, the schools, the corps of road- and bridge-building engineers, the armed forces – everywhere, in fact, except the foreign service and the finance ministry, two impregnable domains that remained in the hands of conservative Catholics. No matter. The integration of Jews into French society was so successful that Paris was widely regarded, especially by Jews in eastern Europe, as the New Jerusalem – until the Dreyfus Affair erupted and split French society in two when it began in 1894. On the pro-Jewish side of that watershed event were most intellectuals and artists and socialists as well as Republicans, those Positivists who believed in Science and Progress and had inherited the universalist ideals of the Revolution. On the other, more racist side were die-hard monarchists, representatives of the old rural Catholic France of traditional values, as well as soldiers who were still smarting from the defeat of France in 1870 at the hands of the Prussians.

Ironically, Alfred Dreyfus, though a Jew, was himself a dedicated French patriot and a captain of good standing in the army, assigned to the general staff (a sign of supreme confidence). He was from a prosperous family based in the town of Mulhouse in Alsace, which was seized and occupied by the Germans after the Franco-Prussian War of 1870. Dreyfus and his family preferred to move to Paris rather than to live under the Prussian yoke. And Dreyfus himself burned with a desire to see vengeance wreaked on the Prussian oppressor. But on 15 October 1894 he was suddenly arrested and imprisoned – having been accused of betraying military secrets to the Prussians.

In December of that year he was convicted by a military court and sent for life to the Devil's Island penal colony in French Guiana. The trial was hasty, emotional and full of juridical errors. The accusation was based on the evidence of a memorandum stolen from the German embassy in Paris (despite the fact that the writing did not resemble Dreyfus's). The dossier that supposedly inculpated Dreyfus was kept classified and secret. The main 'evidence' against Dreyfus was of course the simple fact that he was a Jew. Anti-Semites were quick to point out that he belonged to the same tribe as Judas (no matter that Christ himself belonged to the very same 'tribe'). Like Judas, the bigots claimed, Dreyfus had turned traitor for money alone. They also wrote, 'The scum wasn't French. We had understood everything by his deed, by his looks, by his face.' Maurice Barrès, an ultranationalist writer, made a notorious declaration: 'That Dreyfus is capable of treachery I conclude from his race.'

Dreyfus's brother Mathieu immediately stopped working and devoted himself night and day, year in and year out, to restoring Alfred's reputation. Most Christians assumed his guilt and most Jews were afraid to meddle in the affair, but Mathieu hired a new lawyer, found a handwriting expert who exculpated Alfred, chanced upon a stranger who recognized the writing as that of another military man, pressed for a presidential pardon, and enlisted the aid of a powerful Jewish politician, Joseph Reinach. It was Reinach who published a pamphlet in 1896 that claimed that Dreyfus had been condemned because of his religion alone. 'It was because he was a Jew that he was arrested, it was because he was a Jew that he was judged, it was as a Jew that he was sentenced, and it is because he was a Jew that no one can invoke on his behalf the voice of justice and truth . . .'

In 1896 another soldier, Major Georges Picquart, proved that the memorandum had been written not by Dreyfus but by a certain Major

Marie Charles Esterhazy, the scion of an old Hungarian family. Yet Esterhazy was acquitted and Picquart was imprisoned. A vocal, liberal part of the population called for a retrial of Dreyfus. On 13 January 1898 Émile Zola published an open letter, 'J'accuse', directed against the army's general staff. Zola was tried for slander and was forced to flee to England.

Now the defenders of Dreyfus included not only just a few Jewish friends but also the famous writer Anatole France, the leading doctors of the Pasteur Institute and important professors at the Sorbonne. Professor Émile Durkheim, the most celebrated sociologist of the day, took up the cause, as did Marcel Proust (whose mother was Jewish). The League for Human Rights was born out of this difficult moment, as was Zionism. Theodor Herzl, the Paris correspondent of a Viennese newspaper, had been so alarmed by anti-Semitism in France, the cradle of democracy, that he was inspired by the prophetic idea of a Jewish state.

Then, in September 1898, it was proved that the only piece of evidence against Dreyfus in the 'secret military dossier' had been faked by another French officer, Major Joseph Henry of the general staff, who confessed, was imprisoned and committed suicide. Presumably Henry, by forging documents, had hoped to defend the honour of the army. At this, the government ordered a retrial of Dreyfus, and he was called back from Devil's Island. Once more he was found guilty, but he was pardoned by the President of the Republic. Alfred's brother Mathieu urged the captain to accept the presidential pardon, even if it didn't proclaim his innocence. At least it would save him from death due to harsh prison conditions and give him time to mount a further campaign. Mathieu took the broken Alfred to Provence, where he nursed him back to health.

At last in 1906 the Cour de cassation, the Supreme Court of Appeal, found Dreyfus innocent. He was given the Legion of Honour and named the head of a battalion. In 1930 the publication of the secret notebooks of a German military attaché proved that Dreyfus was innocent and Esterhazy and others were guilty of selling secrets to the Prussians. In the same year Mathieu died and, according to instructions left by the deceased, a simple prayer was read by a rabbi – 'in French'.

Throughout the period between the wars, two tendencies in France became more exaggerated – on one side the integration and gradual social ascension of Jews, and on the other the ever-growing virulence of far-right anti-Semites who'd first hammered out their positions and their rhetoric during the Dreyfus Affair. This contrast became dramatically marked in the 1930s. The worldwide depression made citizens of every country, including France, wary of immigrants who might compete for jobs with native-born workers, many of whom were already unemployed. When Hitler was voted chancellor in 1934 and shortly thereafter dissolved the government, thousands of German Jews fled to France, where they were given a mixed welcome – hostility from fearful workers and far-right parties, such as the Action Française, and generosity and help from the established Jewish community.

The strife over the status of Jews in France became polarized when Léon Blum was elected prime minister in 1936 – the first Jew to hold the highest office in the land. The verbal attacks against Blum finally led to physical violence when a group of right-wing toughs attacked him and nearly turned over his car when he was driving through the Place Maubert. Blum – who'd been a journalist and writer and a friend to Proust – was arrested by the Germans and sent to a camp in 1943. His high office saved his life, but not that of his brother René, who died at Auschwitz in 1942.

In France, as in Germany before Hitler, the population was nearly perfectly divided between voters on the left and those on the right, which led to open conflicts – and intense struggles over the status of Jews. Nevertheless, the long-coming but eventual success of the Dreyfusard faction and the exoneration of Dreyfus himself had re-assured most French Jews that France was still the most liberal country in the world, the true heir to the ideals of the Revolution. This confidence, as it turned out, was tragically misplaced. One quarter of all French Jews were transported to the death camps in Germany and died in transit or in the gas chambers.

The *flâneur* wanders to the Parc Monceau in the eighth arrondissement, just a stroll north and east of the Arc de Triomphe and the Champs-Elysées. Proust lived near here when he was growing up on the rue de Courcelles, at number 45; his neighbours included Camille Saint-Saëns (at 83 *bis*), the composer of *Samson and Delilah*, and Colette, who in 1896 moved with her first husband to number 93, where she conducted a salon amid her sleek Art Nouveau furnishings. Many of the great Jewish families also built houses on the Parc, which was a luxurious, landscaped site, replete with reflecting ponds, little hills and Greek temples; the Corinthian columns clustered around a pool are a leftover from an earlier eighteenth-century garden (the columns are known as the Naumachie).

Developed by a Jewish banker, Emile Pereire, after 1860, the modern park was surrounded by the sumptuous mansions of such Jewish million-aires as the Rothschilds, the Meniers and the Milanese financiers the Cernuschis; today the Cernuschi mansion houses a museum dedicated to their collection of Asian art. The founder of Zionism, Theodor Herzl, lived at number 8 rue de Monceau from 1891 to 1894.

The most impressive museum – and one that tells a melancholy tale – is the Musée Nissim de Camondo. It is located at 63 rue de Monceau and presents a sober, almost sombre façade to the street. Although it resembles the Petit Trianon at Versailles, it was built only in 1911. The owner, Moïse de Camondo, had torn down the family mansion (which had been put up in 1866), in order to construct this copy of an eighteenth-century town house – the ideal setting for his outstanding collection of furniture from the reigns of Louis XV and Louis XVI. Ironically, Camondo, whose own family would be entirely wiped out by the Holocaust, was attracted to the refined furniture, china, rugs and fabrics of an élite that itself was largely destroyed by its enemies.

Although this museum is little known, it houses a collection in its domain only slightly less impressive than those of the Frick Museum in New York and the Wallace in London. And because Camondo left behind instructions that every object must remain where he'd put it when he was living in the house, the whole has a unique lived-in feeling. None of the rooms is huge – which is appropriately in the spirit of the eighteenth century, an epoch that prized intimacy over grandeur, and comfort over magnificence.

The Camondos were a family of Jewish bankers who had been established in Constantinople for centuries but who were first mentioned in Ottoman records only towards the end of the eighteenth century. Temporarily in disfavour, the family fled the Ottoman Empire for Trieste in 1782. They prospered in Italy, where they were ennobled (King Victor Emmanuel II made them counts in 1867), but by the beginning of the nineteenth century some members of the family were back in Constantinople, where they founded a bank and acquired extensive real-estate holdings in Galata, the European quarter. By the mid-nineteenth century the Camondos were internationally known as 'the Rothschilds of the East'.

Although the Ottomans had passed reform laws declaring the equality of all religions and ethnic minorities, nevertheless the fate of a banking family depended upon the whims of the sultan or his prime minister – and in the 1860s the Camondos' bank was passed over in favour of a rival establishment. (In 1894 the Constantinople branch of the Camondo bank was closed for ever.) Abraham and Nissim Camondo immediately understood the grave significance of this change and by 1867 had taken definite steps to transfer the family and its bank to Paris, where the Jewish population was the most perfectly integrated one in the world and the most stable.

Paris was the place for a banker to be. Not only was it the capital of one of the three or four greatest empires in the world at the time, it was also undergoing a vast rebuilding – which entailed virtually the invention of modern banking in order to finance it. In seventeen years under Haussmann, Paris increased its population from 1.2 to 1.6 million inhabitants. Twenty thousand houses were torn down and 44,000 others put up. Eleven towns surrounding Paris were annexed to the city. The sound of wreckers and the look of the demolished city (which people compared to the imaginary ruins depicted by Piranesi) was the constant reality of mid-century Paris. To no less extent the ousting of the poor, the dramatic rise in rents and the colossal fortunes made by building speculators were the stuff of the social history of the day. Proust got it wrong – he imagined that it was the First World War that destroyed the old social hierarchy, but in fact it was the Second Empire. The rise of his own family (his mother being from a family of Jewish stockbrokers enriched under Napoleon III, and his father a Christian from a village near Chartres who rose to become a famous professor of medicine) is in fact a phenomenon of the Emperor's reign.

The Camondos were quickly integrated, by friendship, and sometimes by marriage, with the leading Jewish families – the Rothschilds, to be sure, but also the family headed by the Pereire brothers, as well as the Fould family and the Cahen d'Anvers family. Nissim Camondo moved to Paris in 1868 and his brother Abraham the following year. They bought adjacent properties along the rue de Monceau from Emile Pereire, who was parcelling out the entire Parc Monceau area. Almost immediately the Camondo brothers were attending the opera with their wives and children, furnishing grandiose quarters and buying fine horses and carriages. At their parties they distributed jewels as party favours to the female guests. They adapted themselves quickly to Parisian ways, but they never denied their Turkish – nor their Jewish – origins.

But modern French history is turbulent. The Franco-Prussian war of 1870, which ended with the French defeat and the collapse of Napoleon III's reign, resulted in the brief flourishing of a far-left commune that seized Paris from March through May 1871. The communards burned the Hôtel de Ville, the Tuileries Palace and other government buildings. In a shoot-out with national forces, some 20,000 renegades were killed and another 38,000 arrested after a last-ditch stand in Montmartre.

The Camondos fled to London during this prolonged violence, but they were soon back in Paris, floating the gigantic loans needed to pay the Prussians the war reparations they demanded.

Abraham's son Isaac was the quintessential Parisian man-about-town. He seems to have stepped right out of an Offenbach operetta, complete with his straw boater, his handlebar moustache, his 'fleeing chin', as the French call it *(menton fuyant)*, his wing-tipped collar, rose boutonnière and gold watch chain. He never married but he surrounded himself with dancers and singers from the opera and other *demi-mondaines* (the Palais Garnier opera house, looking like a giant gilded inkwell, was inaugurated in 1875 and quickly became one of his haunts). In fact one of his greatest ambitions was to become known as a composer. After his uncle Nissim and his father Abraham died in the late 1880s, Isaac liquidated his holdings in the family bank and devoted himself exclusively to his artistic pursuits, and to chasing skirts.

Isaac was one of the first and most convinced Wagnerians in Paris, although Wagner was seldom performed in Paris after the Prussians conquered France in 1870. Nevertheless Isaac, accompanied by Léo Delibes (the composer of *Coppélia* and *Lakmé*), made the pilgrimage to Wagner's own opera house at Bayreuth in 1876, the year it was inaugurated, and he returned six years later to hear *Parsifal*. Despite his reverence for (the fiercely anti-Semitic) Wagner, Isaac's own output was closer to the salon music of Delibes with its cloying harmonies and suave melodies. Isaac wrote an opera, *The Clown*, which was finally premiered (at the composer's expense) on 24 April 1906 at a private theatre. The opera was politely reviewed by evasive critics, and praised by the society women who made up Isaac's circle, especially the Countess Greffuhle, the model for Proust's Duchesse de Guermantes.

Elizabeth Greffuhle wrote to the composer:

I want to thank you for the very great artistic pleasure that your work, *The Clown*, brought me. I found in it qualities of sincerity, truth, life, movement – daring perhaps but certainly true and because of that even touching. It seemed to me that there were cuts to be made in the second part . . . The Grand-Duchess Wladimir spoke to me again yesterday evening of *The Clown* and wishes to congratulate you again for the pleasure that she had while listening to your work.

As a music-lover, Isaac put up a substantial sum towards the building of the Théâtre des Champs-Elysées on the Avenue Montaigne, which opened in 1913 – two years after Isaac's death. The theatre, which was recently restored and where concerts and operas are still performed, was the place where Stravinsky's *Rite of Spring* was first staged during the inaugural season, unleashing a storm of protest and consecrating the composer – and the ballet impresario Diaghilev – with a very Parisian *succès de scandale*.

But Isaac's most lasting legacy (even if his name has largely been forgotten) was as an art collector. He bought four hundred Japanese prints at the height of the vogue for them, and he began collecting the Impressionists when they were turning out their most characteristic work and before they'd been accepted by the public. He owned thirty paintings and pastels by Degas and important works by Monet, Sisley, Pissarro and Renoir and by such Post-Impressionists as Van Gogh, Toulouse-Lautrec and Matisse. In 1897 (at the height of the Dreyfus Affair) Isaac and another Jewish patron of the arts, Edmond de Rothschild, joined such aristocrats as the Count Greffuhle and Prince Roland Bonaparte to create the Society of the Friends of the Louvre. Even during his lifetime Isaac made substantial donations to the Louvre, and after his death he left the state museum sixty major Impressionist works.

At first the museum hesitated to accept the donation, since the absolute merit of the Impressionists was far from determined and, moreover, the Louvre had a rule against hanging works by painters who'd not been dead at least ten years (Degas would not die until 1917, for instance). The collection was of such obvious beauty, however, that after some hesitation it was accepted and a few years later displayed. Today Camondo's paintings hang in the Musée d'Orsay, though no longer as a separate collection, and his other belongings are scattered in the Louvre and the Musée Guimet of Asian art. (By the personally modest terms of his will, they were to be kept in their own three rooms at the Louvre only for fifty years.) Given his love of the opera house, it is no surprise to see that Isaac was especially attracted to Degas' paintings of dancers.

It was Isaac's cousin Moïse who built the Musée Camondo. He was known as a *bon viveur* who loved good wines, good food, fine horses and beautiful women. He married one – Irène Cahen d'Anvers, who as a child had modelled for a portrait by Renoir, and whose father was one of the leading Jewish bankers of Paris (originally of Trieste, ennobled by the Pope). Moïse, as head of the family, recognized he had the responsibility for perpetuating its name, and he was more than satisfied when Irène gave birth to a son, Nissim, and a daughter, Béatrice. Having discharged her dynastic duties, Irène promptly fell in love with the Italian in charge of the stables, Count Sampiere. By 1897 she'd officially separated from Moïse and was living openly with the Italian count: she was legally divorced from Moïse by the beginning of 1902. Divorce, which had been legalized only twenty years earlier, was still considered scandalous. The following year Irène was at last married to her count.

Moïse took the divorce very hard. He retreated from the social world and devoted himself to his children – and to his collection of eighteenth-century art and furniture. He withdrew from business as well and put his fortune into extremely safe government stocks and bonds. In that way he was quite unlike the Rothschilds, who were increasing their power and fortune generation after generation.

Perhaps Moïse and Isaac, once the older generation of bankers had died, felt free to indulge in an epicurianism for which they were better suited. Certainly Moïse, when he wasn't travelling with his children from one fashionable spa to another or hunting at his house in the country (which he named Béatrice in honour of his daughter), could think of little else besides the next big auction of eighteenth-century things, whether it was to take place in Paris or London. Perhaps, as his biographers have suggested, his collecting was originally a 'strategy for integration' into the aristocratic Christian society around him, since a taste for the eighteenth century had been fashionable ever since the Goncourt brothers (Edmond and Jules, famous novelists and diarists of the day) and the Empress Eugénie had worked up a passion for it. But what started out as a strategy soon became a personal obsession.

Today Paris is far less important as a centre for the sale of traditional art than London or New York, mainly due to French laws that give the state the right to pre-empt the exportation of paintings, sculptures and pieces of furniture. Whatever is deemed irreplaceable can be refused an export licence – which obviously cools the ardour of international collectors. At the turn of the century, however, Paris was still the world centre of such sales, and Moïse participated not only in auctions but was also well served by Jacques and Arnold Seligmann, two of the leading antique dealers of the day, who had galleries not only in Paris but also in New York.

Throughout the First World War Moïse was buying furniture for his new house on the rue de Monceau – couches, armchairs, screens, sketches of the hunts of Louis XV by Jean-Baptiste Oudry, round tables, oval tables, tables to be set in corners, tiny desks, sewing tables, rolltop desks, chests of drawers – all fashioned from the rarest woods, signed by the greatest masters and decorated with porcelain inlays or gilt bronze details or composed of marquetry made from pearwood, rosewood, sycamore and boxwood. One small room in the museum is devoted to nothing but ornithological china – that is, dishes and cups and plates and serving plates manufactured at Sèvres in the 1780s and decorated with the many different birds featured in a book by the great naturalist Buffon. Also featured are petrified wood vases that belonged to Marie Antoinette, silver from Catherine II of Russia, a green marble console from the palace in Warsaw – all royal spoils for a discerning collector.

The neo-classical house at 63 rue de Monceau, begun in 1911, took four years and forty men to build. When it was being finished, Moïse's son Nissim was fighting for France. Tall, dashing, mustachioed, trailing clouds of his favourite scent, Eau de Cologne de Russie, Nissim served heroically as a pilot, photographing enemy installations from the air and verifying that French artillery was hitting the desired targets. In September 1917, while on a photographic reconnaissance trip behind enemy lines, he exchanged fire with a German plane – and both planes went down in flames.

Moïse was devastated. He liquidated his share in the family businesses, including real-estate holdings in Turkey, and decided to devote the rest of his life to his collection, which would at his death form the basis of a museum dedicated to the memory of Nissim. Isolated by his growing deafness, Moïse seldom received guests other than people in the museum world, and then but rarely. His daughter Béatrice (who married Léon Reinach, the scion of the prominent Dreyfusard family, in 1918, the year of the Armistice) fully accepted her father's plans for the museum, though it meant that most of his fortune would be diverted into it.

Moïse died in 1935. His daughter made sure that his plans for the museum were faithfully executed. Like her father, she almost never ventured into society and lived a life devoted to her stepfather's trade – riding horses. She and her husband drifted apart. She converted to Catholicism. The next war came along and her husband pleaded with her to flee France, but she stubbornly continued to ride her horse every day in the Bois de Boulogne, often accompanied by a German officer. As a Catholic convert and as a Camondo, she must have felt immune. But in the summer of 1942 she and her children, Fanny and Bertrand, were arrested by the authorities and sent to Drancy, a camp just outside Paris, where they were joined by Léon Reinach. On the morning of 10 March 1943 Béatrice arrived at Auschwitz. She'd been preceded by the rest of her family – Léon, Fanny and Bertrand. They never returned. The Camondos, who had contributed so much to the cultural life of France, had been entirely extinguished, and the French authorities had done nothing to save them. Their family motto had been 'Faith and Charity'. Perhaps it was telling that they had made no mention of the third traditional virtue, Hope.

Today there are few reminders of the Camondo family in their museum. The weak winter light enters through the many windows and lays another thin layer of varnish on these splendid rooms, in which every detail is authentically eighteenth century – everything from the rugs to those tiny writing desks called *Bonheur-du-jour*, the carved and gilded fireplaces and the rich tones of the wood panelling. In one room upstairs there are two glass cases containing the only personal memorabilia – an announcement of *The Clown* is displayed as well as a condolence letter from Proust after the death of Nissim in 1917. There's also an invitation to a Camondo banquet that was sent to Thomas Edison in 1889.

And there's a book of prayers in Hebrew, printed in 1839, that belonged to the patriarch of the family, Solomon Abraham – the only sign of the family's Jewish origins amid so much royal splendour.

CHAPTER FOUR

PARIS HAS COUNTLESS small and bizarre museums, little corners where someone's bid for immortality goes unnoticed – one might say a neglected shrine to a forgotten god. Or sometimes the museum caters to a perfectly real and valid taste, but one not shared by too many people.

Take the Musée des Cristalleries de Baccarat at number 30 *bis* rue de Paradis in the tenth arrondissement. It houses the most beautiful historic examples of fine Baccarat and St Louis crystal. (In the spring this museum should be visited just at closing time when night is beginning to fall and the crystals are glowing dimly in the last shreds of daylight.)

Or there's the Museum of Romantic Life, dedicated to the memory of George Sand and her artistic circle, which included Ingres, Delacroix, Liszt and Sand's lover Chopin. It's a house with a quiet garden at number 16 rue Chaptal in the section known as the New Athens (La Nouvelle Athènes in the ninth arrondissement) between the Trinité Church and the Place Blanche, the beginning of Montmartre.

In the Marais there's a museum of hunting (Chasse et Nature). At 380 rue St Honoré there's a museum of eyeglasses (Lunettes et Lorgnettes), which includes among its three thousand objects a pair of brass-rimmed seventeenth-century spectacles in a carved wooden case, as well as a gilded cane with a little telescope inside from the time of Louis XV.

There are museums of perfume, of locksmithery, of palaeobotany, of Madame Curie, of the philosopher Auguste Comte, the pope of Positivism, as well as museums of dermatology, of holography, of anatomy – and of public welfare (Assistance Publique), a good place for seeing gory re-creations of nineteenth-century surgical procedures. At number 5 rue Duroc in the seventh arrondissement there's a museum dedicated to Valentin Haüy, who founded a school for the blind in 1784 (the collection includes maps and globes in relief as well as bronze sculptures fashioned by the blind artist Vidal).

The Flâneur

There are museums of the army, of the poster, of the Middle Ages, of the police – and *two* major museums of fashion, which is not so surprising in the world capital of dress design. There are museums dedicated to Rodin (a great mansion with extensive gardens, filled inside and out with the master's writhing bronzes, including *The Thinker* and *The Gates of Hell* in the front yard). There are museums to Delacroix (his studio is on the small, charming Place de Fürstemberg) and to the obscure painter Jean-Jacques Henner.

I have two favourite museums – one that is closed to the public and one open, the Gustave Moreau Museum. The closed one is the Hôtel de Lauzun on the austerely beautiful quai d'Anjou of the Île St Louis, which is less a museum than a beautifully restored seventeenth-century town-house used by the metropolitan government of Paris for lavish receptions of notables, during which the guests are served by bewigged lackeys. In the spring and summer certain architectural tours of the island are allowed into parts of the house.

Hôtel de Lauzun was built originally in the 1640s by Charles Grüyn,the son of a rich tavern keeper. The interior of the house is made up of room after room that combine fancy, grandeur and intimacy in unusual proportions. The various

123

artists who decorated it seem to have had a horror of a vacuum – every square inch is covered with carved and gilt eagles, shells, sheaves, painted quivers stuffed with arrows, three-dimensional cupids, an allegorical ceiling painting of Spring showing garlands of pink roses draped around masks sprouting horns from the eyes, linked initials (*G* and *M* – that is Grüyn and his wife, Geneviève de Mouy) and 'Michelangelo-Lite' caryatids flanking a bare-breasted Printemps attended by a *putto* with butterfly wings. In another room the ceiling is devoted to the theme of *La Toilette de Vénus*, Venus arraying herself, surrounded by scenes of the loves of the gods.

The rooms aren't large but one side looks down on the Seine through tall casement windows. Mirrors placed here and there strategically catch the pale, cold north light and toss it back and forth.

The history of the house comprises a series of fascinating disasters. Grüyn, the original owner, enjoyed his house only a few years before he was imprisoned for embezzling state funds (he was the supplier of mess rations to the light cavalry and got his hand caught in the till). The next owner was the Count de Lauzun, after whom the house is still named. He had just spent ten years in prison for having dared to court Louis XIV's cousin, La Grande Mademoiselle; now, at last, he was permitted to marry this older, royal and royally disputatious woman. They moved into the Île St Louis house – and fought so bitterly that they separated after three years. (Lauzun gloried in bossing his wife around and would shout at her with more venom than ease of expression, 'Granddaughter of Henri IV, pull off my boots!')

The next owners were the grand-niece of Cardinal Mazarin and the grand-nephew of Cardinal Richelieu. The young man had been so in love with the Mazarin girl that he'd abducted her from a convent. They ran up enormous debts giving lavish parties at the Hôtel de Lauzun, assuming all along that they'd be inheriting the title and estate of the Marquis de Richelieu's older brother. But the older brother suddenly and against all odds produced an heir and the young, extravagant couple were ruined. The husband sank into debauchery and his wife ran away to join her mother in London, where she dazzled everyone with her dissipations – and her beauty, depite the fact that her father had pulled her front teeth when she was a girl in order to discourage all potential suitors.

The next few owners were considerably less colourful and met less tragic fates; one of them had the merit of safeguarding the house against depredations during the Revolution. In 1842 the *hôtel* came back into history when it was bought by Baron Jérôme Pichon, who restored it and rented out rooms with a river view to the young poet Charles Baudelaire. His small apartment was on the second floor. He had come into a small inheritance after his father's death and now he ran up considerable debts furnishing his flat with antiques from Arondel – the unscrupulous shop owner on the ground floor who took advantage of the young poet's impulsiveness and naïveté.

Baudelaire was perhaps the first performance artist in history. At least he was one of the first to live out his aesthetics, to make his home décor, his clothes, even his way of moving, consistent with his poetry. As the portrait photographer Nadar recalled, 'Monsieur Baudelaire was gloved in pink and proceeded in his walk by little jerks, like a wooden marionette, seeming to choose each place where he would step, as if walking between eggs.' He was the great apostle of dandyism, and he thought nothing of spending so much of his fortune on curious medieval furniture, Rhine wine, emerald-coloured goblets, loose robes and rich foods that when he died in 1867 he still owed money to shopkeepers for these extravagances of his early twenties. In his letters to friends from this period Baudelaire frequently talks about the purchase of a Japanese print, a writing desk, a drawing or bits of bric-à-brac long before such bizarre objects bought randomly were *à la mode*. As he wrote, his ideal was 'the man who is rich, idle, even blasé, who has no other occupation than to run on the path towards happiness; the man brought up in luxury . . .'

Although Baudelaire later suffered – in his dispute over the control of his fortune with his stepfather, General Aupick, in his amorous disappointments with women, in his battles with censors over his collection of poems, *The Flowers of Evil*, and in his struggle with syphilis – nevertheless in his years at the Hôtel de Lauzun (which was known as the Hôtel Pimodan in his day, after a more recent owner), the poet was entirely happy. His mistress, an actress named Jeanne Duval who was one-quarter black, was living just a few blocks away. Jeanne was the one whom Baudelaire addressed in his poetry as a strange deity brown as night (*'bizarre déité brune comme les nuits'*). Her rooms were on the rue de la Femme-sans-Tête ('the Headless Woman', now the rue Le Regrattier); the street was named after a sign in front of an inn that showed a woman without a head and the slogan 'Everything is good', meaning that all was well when one dealt with a headless woman. Baudelaire was writing some of the most important poems in these years, 1843 and 1844 – according to some experts, the majority of the poems that would eventually appear in *Les Fleurs du Mal*.

But by September 1844 the party was over. The poet's mother, dismayed that her son had spent 44,500 gold francs in two years, had the rest of his fortune placed in the hands of a guardian who would dole it out in minuscule monthly sums. Nine months later the humiliated poet attempted suicide by knifing himself (he wrote that suicide is the 'only sacrament in the religion of dandyism'), but he failed to do himself in and was nursed back to health by Jeanne Duval. After that he limped home to his mother and lived with her. His glorious years on the Île St Louis were over.

The poet Théodore de Banville, writing some forty years later, remembered fondly a visit to Baudelaire at the Hôtel de Lauzun. When Baudelaire lived on the Île St Louis, he'd just come back from a trip to Mauritius and Réunion, two islands in the Indian Ocean. He'd brought back exotic recipes from his travels and shared them with Banville, his best friend at the time. He spoke lovingly of his stay on a mountain in Réunion where he had lived with a native woman who prepared him highly spiced ragouts in a giant cauldron of polished brass while little black children danced around it howling. His apartment in Paris was decorated with a glossy wallpaper covered with red and black branches and at the one big window were draperies of a heavy, ancient damask. Baudelaire had scratched the lower panes so that only the sky could be seen and the expensive river view was occluded. On the walls hung the series of Delacroix's *Hamlet* lithographs, unframed but protected by glass, and the same artist's painting of *The Women of Algiers*. The furniture – armchairs covered with grey slipcovers, divans and an oval table in walnut – was all immense, fashioned for a race of titans.

When Banville remarked out loud that there were no books in sight, Baudelaire showed him thirty beautifully bound volumes lying one on top of another in a closet – old, ornate books of poetry in Old French and Latin. When these things were hidden away, there were no dictionaries, no inkwells or pens or pen-sharpeners or blotter, no books nor paper in sight – nothing to recall the sordid business of being a writer.

It was at the Hôtel de Lauzun that Le Club des

Edmund White

Hachichins held its meetings. Here a group of artistic men – including the writers Balzac, Gautier, and Baudelaire and the painters Édouard Manet, Honoré Daumier and Constantin Guys – came together with a few women for long evenings of music . . . and eating hashish (for they appeared to eat it in the form of a greenish jelly). Their host, the minor painter Fernand Boissard, was independently wealthy and lived on the main, princely floor, where he had a clavichord reputedly covered with paintings by Watteau and other elegant furnishings that went well with the painted, carved and gilded walls and doorways. When stoned, Boissard would play the violin, or arrange for musicians to perform a Beethoven trio or one by Mozart.

One visitor, Paul Guilly, recalled that Boissard

. . . was a voluptuary, refined man, opposed to all annoying, unwelcome guests. If his highest pleasure was to entertain, he knew how to select his visitors; you couldn't drop in on him uninvited, but once you were admitted into the inner circle you could do or say what you liked. He surrounded himself with artists who shared his tastes and pretty girls who weren't stuffy nor for that matter oblivious to spiritual or artistic matters. He loved above all dinners among tried and

true friends, intimate evenings where one teased
out the meanings of a paradox between a tune on
the harpsichord and the stanzas of a poem.

Théophile Gautier wrote a highly coloured account of the first time he attended one of the
monthly meetings of Le Club des Hachichins. He
recalled that it was night and the fog was so
heavy that every object was blurred behind 'torn
cotton with holes in it'. A cold rain was falling
and Gautier's coachman could scarcely make out
the marble plaque that gave the name of the
townhouse. An old gatekeeper opened the heavy
entrance door and indicated the way with a bony
finger.

Suddenly the writer was in one of those immense stairwells built in the era of Louis XIV,
inside which a whole modern house could be
easily fitted. The statue of an Egyptian chimera
held aloft a single candle. Thinking of the cour-
tiers of the seventeenth century in their wigs and
laces, Gautier felt seriously underdressed. Upstairs he rang a bell and was admitted to a large
room illuminated only at one end; the visitor
realized he'd just stepped back two centuries into
the past.

A doctor was in charge of the hashish. He came
forward with a tray burdened with the green

jelly. After the guests ate it, Turkish coffee was passed around. Having started with the last thing to be served at a typical French dinner, they then sat down to a meal served in the normal way. The glasses and dishes, however, were strange, exotic – mismatched plates from China, Japan and Saxony, crystal goblets from Venice. Under the influence of the drug, the water tasted like wine and the beef like raspberries. By the end of the meal Gautier felt he was going mad. Hallucinations, which had swept over him in waves during the dinner, now became a permanent if ever-fluctuating part of his perception for the rest of the evening.

All the signs of being totally, deliriously, even dangerously stoned, so well known to my reader, were already familiar to the arty denizens of the Hôtel de Lauzun. They fell about laughing, then an unspeakable fear seized them, to be followed by a melting love of all humanity or by total immersion in a picture book. Movement became slow and sticky, the size of the rooms expanded dramatically, a sense of the epic and the magnificent distorted the feeling of the gathering, to be replaced by a repulsed gaze on the grotesque faces of the other revellers. Everything was so distorted – and so appealing to the imagination – that no wonder Gautier's word

for such a soirée was a 'fantasia'. Did he know
that a fantasia was also a free-form piece of
music given over to improvisation? Or a gala
military display on horseback in Morocco, one
that involved thundering attacks of squadron
after squadron of cavalry with crack equitation
skills, velvet and gilt costumes and flowing
robes, fine stallions, a band and drums and even
dancing, the whole blurred by the smoke from
the open fires where the coming feast was being
prepared?

To be sure, Balzac inspected the green jelly
carefully and even took the various Middle Eastern drug implements in his hands and asked all
his customary material-gathering questions – but
didn't touch the hashish, fearful of losing control
over his steely will or supple mind. The Hashish
Club probably met no more than eight or nine
times. Nor is there any evidence that Baudelaire
himself tried the drug more than once or twice; in
any event he compared it unfavourably to wine,
which he thought was more 'democratic' because
cheaper and more widely available (like Oscar
Wilde, Baudelaire was both a 'socialist' and an
aesthetic snob). To be precise, he praised both
wine and hashish for promoting 'the excessive
poetic development of mankind', but he pointed
out that

wine exalts the will, hashish annihilates it. Wine is a support to the body, hashish is a weapon for suicide. Wine makes people good and friendly. Hashish isolates. One is hard-working, so to speak, whereas the other is essentially lazy. Why would anyone bother to work, to plough, to write, to make anything at all, when with one blow he can attain paradise? Wine is for those people who work and deserve to drink it. Hashish belongs to the category of solitary pleasures; it is made for the unhappy idle. Wine is useful, it produces fruitful results. Hashish is useless and dangerous.

Perhaps Baudelaire's imagination was as stirred by the atmosphere of the Hôtel de Lauzun as by hashish itself. He and Gautier also revelled in the legend that the word *hashish* was linked to the word *assassin*; Gautier related the tale of the 'Oriental' despot who turned his men into death-defying, insanely fearless marauders (or assassins) by keeping them constantly stoned on hashish.

Or perhaps Baudelaire was stimulated by his companions, including a striking, gender-bending young woman known as Pomaré (her real name was Elise Sergent). 'La Pomaré', as Baudelaire called her, dressed as a 'gentleman' (the English word was used) in white tie and black cutaway and black trousers and white overcoat. She carried a cane in her white-gloved hand. She was a good fellow and good company – unless she spied a *bourgeoise* on entering a restaurant. If, for example, she should see the wife of a notary seated with her husband, she'd fly into a rage and start singing her favourite song – which was all about a general of the Italian army squatting on the ground and scratching his balls, which prompts an elegant virgin to tell him he's nothing but an arse . . . The Pomaré was tall and svelte, with a flat chest, a ready wit and such a straightforward manner that Baudelaire called her 'my pal with hips'. The Pomaré lived in the Hôtel de Lauzun and Baudelaire lusted after her (at least he was stirred by the idea of such an unfussy woman) as much as he esteemed her.

An equally strong aura surrounds the Gustave Moreau Museum.

Moreau's house attracted both real and fictional characters. Oscar Wilde's Dorian Gray moons over Moreau's paintings. Proust wrote of Moreau's house in 'Notes on the Mysterious World of Gustave Moreau'. Des Esseintes, the hero of J. K. Huysmans' bible of decadence,

Edmund White

Against Nature (*À rebours*), gazes at Moreau's works lovingly, these androgynes and pale youths and bejewelled enchantresses who summarize the Decadent movement – work executed by a man who was a hermit, but a knowing, worldly one. (As Degas said, 'He's a hermit who knows the train schedule.') Huysmans' male characters were masochistic ephebes (St Sebastian is a favourite, wilting subject), his women were cruel beauties (he painted Salomé obsessively, as she slobbers over John the Baptist's severed head), and all of them resembled one another. Cézanne had an allergy to him and attributed Moreau's unhealthiness to his haunting museums rather than observing nature. When Moreau said to Degas, 'You claim that you're going to restore art through dance?', Degas replied, 'And you, do you think you're going to renew it through jewellery?'

Moreau left his house in the ninth arrondissement at 14 rue de La Rochefoucauld to the French state, although the state hesitated to accept such a huge collection of unfinished works. Even before he died in 1898 he was already planning to turn his family *hôtel* into a shrine to his own memory. For years he'd been hoarding his paintings and sketches, refusing to sell them, even though they commanded very high prices and his patrons included Napoleon III's cousin Jérôme Napoléon. The museum today, seldom visited, is hung ceiling to floor with his weird, hectic but paradoxically monotonous canvases and features even a gilt altarpiece that includes nine strange panels to illustrate Moreau's warped vision of *The Life of Humanity*. There are so many sketches that Moreau has placed them between glass leaves that hang along the walls and open up on hinges like the pages of a giant book, a display idea of his own invention.

Today Moreau – despite the best efforts of his defenders – attracts little attention. When the Metropolitan Museum in New York, for instance, hosted a major Moreau exhibition in 1999 (one that had begun a year earlier in Paris at the Grand Palais), museum-goers stayed in the next gallery looking at the Van Goghs in a show devoted to the mad Dutchman's patron Dr Gachet. Gustave Moreau is camp without the humour, pastiche without the sweep and drama of the truly good copies of the classics, Decadence without the bruised colour and haunting invention of an Odilon Redon or the sinuous lines and striking compositions (and scary lubricity) of an Aubrey Beardsley.

As early as 1900 the tide had already turned against Moreau. The art critic Gustave Geoffroy remarked, on coming out of the museum, on the way all the canvases looked as if they'd been worked up with the same application, the same approach, the same patience. The great poet and travel writer (and occasional art critic) Victor Segalen could find nothing to praise after his visit other than the made-up, screwy archaeology used for Moreau's settings – part Mesopotamian, part Hindu, part proto-Hellenic . . . Paul Valéry muttered that the paintings were 'dull and grey as a pavement'. The old Degas so thoroughly disliked his visit that he decided against a museum for his own works.

Moreau's museum quickly became such a quiet backwater that it was an ideal place for a lovers' rendezvous. It was there that Suzanne Valadon – who'd been a circus acrobat and model for Toulouse-Lautrec, Degas and Renoir before becoming a celebrated painter and single mother (her son was the painter Utrillo) – first arranged a romantic tryst in 1910 with her young lover André Utter. And it was there that the young and impressionable André Breton formed his taste in women, as he later wrote:

The discovery of the Gustave Moreau Museum when I was sixteen conditioned ever after the way in which I loved. It was there that through certain faces and female poses I had a revelation of beauty and love. The 'type' of these women has probably blocked out all others from me; I was totally bewitched . . . Myths, which were bodied forth here as nowhere else, must have played a role. This woman who without changing a single feature is in turn Salomé, Helen of Troy, Delilah, the Chimera and Semele took hold of me as through a vague embodiment. She . . . fixed her features in the realm of the eternal.

In 1864 Moreau made his name by hanging at the state-sponsored Salon his first 'masterpiece', *Oedipus and the Sphinx* (a work that today is owned by the Metropolitan). For several years previously Moreau had not shown – he'd also spent two years in Rome absorbing the spirit of the ancients. Previous to this exhibition the whole status of historical painting had been challenged by the new Realism, as practised by painters such as Courbet and Manet. Yet *Oedipus and the Sphinx* was widely regarded as a resuscitation and vindication of the older genre. Maxime Du Camp – Flaubert's faithful sidekick – announced that 'Moreau has left nothing to chance; everything he has done, he has willed to do like this. Each part of his painting is reasoned and pondered with serious concern.' This judgement, that

Moreau had left nothing to chance and had *willed* into existence even the most minute detail, was echoed by several other critics. Manet's magnificent *Angels at the Tomb of Christ* hung in the same room as Moreau's painting, but Manet was either ignored or compared unfavourably to Moreau.

Prince Napoléon bought Moreau's painting through an intermediary for 8,000 francs (perhaps he feared the price would be higher if Moreau knew the identity of the royal collector). He tired of it rather quickly, however, and soon enough it ended up in the collection of a rich American in Rome, William H. Herriman. Young painters such as Odilon Redon saw the *Oedipus* as encouragement to pursue a course outside the mainstream; as he recalled, 'When I saw *Oedipus and the Sphinx* for the first time, when I was young, naturalism was at its height, and how the work soothed me!' Gautier praised it for combining the moodiness of Hamlet with the style of Mantegna, who'd outlined his figures in the same way with a black line that emphasized their sculptural look. Most critics singled out for praise the accuracy of Moreau's historical details; the four griffins on the urn beside Oedipus, for instance, were copied from a print by Piranesi in the series *Antique Vases from the*

Collection of Richard Dalton. Moreau had also borrowed the subject itself as well as some key details from Ingres' 1808 painting *Oedipus Explaining the Riddle of the Sphinx.*

Today it's hard to understand how Moreau's painting was ever taken seriously. Although the bare-breasted female Sphinx has leapt up on Oedipus and dug her lioness claws into his bare flesh, her face looks no more menacing than the young Queen Victoria's as seen in profile on a coin of the realm, and the languid young man looks vaguely pettish as if she has just said something disobliging about his gold gauze halter top, which has slipped fetchingly to reveal a virginal pink nipple. There is no sense that she is threatening his very life instead of one of his sartorial whims. As Degas said, 'He would have us believe the gods wore watch chains.' The background (as one critic put it in describing a later work) is made up of a 'praline landscape' and a 'rock candy mountain'.

Writers made Moreau's reputation, primarily the Parnassian and Symbolist poets, including: the rich Cuban sonneteer José-Maria de Heredia; the high priest of Symbolism, Stéphane Mallarmé; the preposterous exquisite Robert de Montesquiou (the model for Proust's grotesque snob Charlus); and such purple prosateurs as

Oscar Wilde, Huysmans and Jean Lorrain (a painted old queen with whom Proust had duelled for 'insinuating' he might be homosexual; the fact that they were both queer – and the dispute ludicrous – didn't occur to either of them). This band responded appreciatively to Moreau's priestly airs, his skinny, long-haired, sulky boys and bloodthirsty, over-the-top dominatrices. (Was it a tactic on Moreau's part that he never revealed to his gay admirers that for many years he had been living with a flesh-and-blood mistress, Alexandrine Dureux?) Proust went so far as to proclaim Moreau a god and his house half church, half rectory. Perhaps sensing that his reputation would die with his writer friends, Moreau objected violently to the charge that he was a 'literary painter'. One composer admired him as well: the young Debussy, who declared his two favourite artists were Botticelli and Moreau.

Moreau's other claim to fame was his reputation as a painting professor at the École des Beaux-Arts, where he instructed the young Rouault and Matisse. Both of them praised his open-mindedness, good taste and general enthusiasm. When Matisse began to paint in his revolutionary, Modernist way, Moreau ardently defended him. Rouault found in him a quickness of wit and a wide curiosity about everything human more characteristic of the Enlightenment than of his own day.

Perhaps his staunchest defenders in the twentieth century were the Surrealists, probably because they were all so eager to follow Breton's party line. Typically, the writer Georges Bataille defended Moreau against the charge of being static by arguing that he was the painter of 'heaviness and sleepiness'. Certainly those two qualities dominate his museum. A narrow staircase leads up from the ground floor and his parents' cramped quarters. Suddenly a mammoth, cathedral-ceiling museum confronts the visitor, a room secluded from the street but given over to the weak, watery light of Paris. A guard is dozing in a chair next to a radiator. A blinking, bewildered Japanese couple are looking with frightened smiles at these naked women fondling unicorns, this somnolent, unsexy Leda on whose head the amorous swan is balancing its beak, this naked Salomé boldly pointing at a flaming bearded head levitating in the gloom. Several canvases have been visibly 'extended' by Moreau, who decided their dimensions were not impressive enough and corrected them by pasting on panels on each side. Others are tattooed with strange arabesques that Moreau intended to enamel later with rich colours but never got around to filling in. A hairless St Sebastian with a prominent 'outie' belly button is staring madly at us as if on acid, his hands bound to the tree behind him but so poorly drawn that it appears he's holding his halo down like a straw boater in a high wind.

Most of the women are heavily robed, whereas most of the young men are naked. Typically, some pale-faced, overdressed muses are walking stiffly away from an etiolated, sulky Apollo sprawling on a raised throne. The crucified Christ is rather furiously cruising a humpy thief on an adjoining cross. The radiator hisses. The guard stirs and swoons back into sleep. Rain falls on the high windows. The Japanese shrug and move on. Moreau once declared, 'I love my art so much that I'll be happy only when I make it for myself alone.' His wish came true.

CHAPTER FIVE

TO BE GAY AND CRUISE is perhaps an extension of the *flâneur*'s very essence, or at least its most successful application. With one crucial difference: the *flâneur*'s promenades are meant to be useless, deprived of any goal beyond the pleasure of merely circulating. Of course a gay man's sorties may end up going unrewarded, but he doesn't set out with that aesthetic disinterestedness – unless sex itself is seen to be pure: artistic and pointless.

The *Spartacus International Gay Guide*, updated every year, directs the gay and lesbian tourist to the bars, saunas and cruisy spots in every city throughout the world and comments on them with an elaborate code of capital and lower-case letters. *AYOR*, for instance, stands for 'At your own risk' and is a warning that danger (queer-bashing, police arrests, pickpockets) may be in the offing. For Paris alone there are some thirty-six closely printed pages of listings, which include cruising places such as particular parks and most of the train stations as well as dark stretches along the Seine or the Canal St Martin.

When I arrived in Paris I was a fairly young-looking forty-three and when I left I was nearly sixty, snowy-haired and jowly. In the beginning I'd cruise along the Seine near the Austerlitz train station under a building that was cantilevered out over the shore on pylons. Or I'd hop over the fence and cruise the pocket park at the end of the Île St Louis, where I lived. There I'd either clatter through the bushes or descend the steps to the quay that wrapped around the prow of the island like the lower deck of a sinking ship. Garlands of ivy dangled down the white walls from the deck above. I kept thinking of those lines in Ezra Pound's Second Canto where a Greek ship is immobilized at sea and transformed by the gods:

> And where was gunwhale, there now was
>   vine-trunk,
> And tenthril where cordage had been,
>   grape-leaves on the rowlocks,
> Heavy vine on the oarshafts,

And, out of nothing, a breathing, hot breath
on my ankles,
Beasts like shadows in glass, a furred tail on
nothingness.

I had to step over the giant rusting rings on the
quayside to which boats could be roped – though
I never saw a boat moored there. When the
bâteaux mouches would swing round the island,
their klieg lights were so stage-set bright that
we'd all break apart and try to rearrange our
clothing. I kept hoping I'd run once more into an
ardent, muscular lad who came home with me
several times but never told me his name or gave
me his number; all this boy would admit to was
that he was kept in great style, in a town house in
the Marais, by a German businessman who
greatly resembled . . . me. (Busman's holiday,
apparently.)

Of course most people, straight and gay, think
that cruising is pathetic or sordid – but for me, at
least, some of my happiest moments have been
spent making love to a stranger beside dark,
swiftly moving water below a glowing city. If
you're a history buff, you can look at men (but
not touch them) in the late afternoon in the
Tuileries Gardens up and down the gravel walk-
way behind the Orangerie. At night the whole

place rocks – or did, at least, when I was still motivated to jump over fences and prowl (illegally) the moonlit pathways between ancient and modern statues or circle the mammoth round pond in which prehistoric carp doze in the ooze and surface in a feeding frenzy only when someone scatters breadcrumbs.

I say 'history buff' because some of the earliest arrests for 'sodomy' or the 'antiphysical' vice (the one that was 'against nature') occurred in the Tuileries. Because of the police records we know that not all gays were aristocrats – as some law-abiders would have liked to think, branding homosexuality as a form of decadence endemic to the privileged and jaded. No, the arrests included married butchers with wives and many children and valets and shopkeepers, music masters and notary's clerks, all caught in the bushes and the act.

The stories about royal and aristocratic decadence undoubtedly started because people in high places could dare to live out their caprices. King Henri III (1551–1589) surrounded himself with his *mignons*, young men known for their astonishing beauty. At a ball the king and his men dressed as women and the women as men. The poet Agrippa d'Aubigné wrote:

At first glance one could scarcely tell
If he was looking at a king-woman or a man-
queen.

The *mignons*, in any case, were sufficiently bi-sexual to duel with one another over the favour of women – and brave enough to defend their monarch when he was attacked during the religious wars between Protestants and Catholics. This theme of bisexuality kept cropping up in the seventeenth century. (Perhaps Latin men, with their strong sense of seduction and their love of family, inevitably travel *à voile et à vapeur,* 'by sail and steam', as bisexuality was – and still is occasionally – called.) A group of nobles who'd gathered around Louis XIV's homosexual brother created a fraternity; they vowed never to touch a woman and even unfurled a flag showing a knight trampling a woman, as St George is pictured trampling the dragon. Despite such insolence, its members were constantly backsliding into covert heterosexuality. So much anxiety about hardening oneself against female charms would be incomprehensible because utterly unnecessary in New York today, for instance. But in the 'Italian Fraternity', as it was called, the third article in their secret constitution read:

If any of the brothers marries he must swear that he did so only to improve his fortunes or because his parents forced him to do so or because he had to produce an heir. He will pronounce an oath at the same time never to love his wife, to sleep with her only until she gives him an heir and that even for such minimal contact he must ask permission, which will be granted him only one day a week.

In the eighteenth century arrests of homosexuals were numerous, but punishments not terribly severe. Aristocrats were usually released at once and other offenders were held no more than two weeks in jail and let go with a warning. Burning at the stake had been the occasional penalty for sodomy in earlier centuries, but that grisly fate had become rare in the eighteenth century. Only seven sodomites were burned to death in Paris between 1714 and 1783, and five of these were guilty of other heinous crimes such as blasphemy or murder. A defrocked monk accused of stabbing a young man who'd rebuffed his advances was the last sodomite to be condemned to the stake, in 1783.

Despite police persecution, nothing could stamp out homosexuality. On the eve of the Revolution nearly forty thousand Parisians were under police surveillance because of their questionable morals. Certain cruising spots had become notorious, especially the gardens of the Tuileries and the Palais Royal. Sodomites and pederasts (as homosexuals were called nearly interchangeably) met regularly in notorious taverns, booked rooms upstairs for sexual assignations, called each other by female names, and aped aristocratic ways.

In 1791 the revolutionary Constituent Assembly overthrew French antisodomy laws – a first anywhere in the world and sure proof of the rejection of Christian values. Napoleon's government inherited this tolerance. During the Empire sodomy may no longer have been on the books, but men were still occasionally arrested for disturbing the peace or committing public acts against decency. Nevertheless, the new regime was measurably more liberal than any preceding government. Before Napoleon crowned himself emperor he ruled France in the Roman style as First Consul. His hand-picked Second Consul was a notorious homosexual, Jean-Jacques de Cambacérès, who incorporated the 1791 measure decriminalizing homosexuality into the new Napoleonic constitution.

When Cambacérès' enemies attempted to pass a law requiring all representatives in Congress to be married, he was forced to give a passionate

Edmund White

speech defending 'bachelorhood'. His eloquence won the day. When Napoleon declared himself emperor he made his beloved Cambacérès the arch-chancellor, though the ruler couldn't restrain himself from teasing his minister. Once Cambacérès excused himself for being late by saying he'd been 'detained by a lady'. Napoleon quipped, 'The next time you must tell this *person* to take his hat, his cane and leave.' (The remark is a bit more subtle in French since the word *personne* is feminine and the possessive pronouns modify 'hat' and 'cane' and don't reveal the person's gender.)

When Napoleon was petitioned to judge harshly a 'ring' of homosexuals arrested in Chartres, the Emperor announced, 'We are not in a country where the law should concern itself with these offences. Nature has seen to it that they are not frequent. The scandal of legal proceedings would only tend to multiply them.'

One of the most open French homosexuals of the nineteenth century was Astolphe de Custine. In his own day he was best known for his book *Russia in 1839*, which sold some 200,000 copies worldwide; it was one of the best accounts of Russia's peculiar destiny ever written. A critic of absolute monarchy, a popular novelist of his day known for his scathing portraits of thinly veiled contemporaries, Custine had a gift for simple, penetrating observations. For instance, he wrote, 'In Louis XIV's century one had a freedom of language dependent on the certainty of being heard only by people who all lived and talked in the same way; there was society, but no public. Today there is a public, but no society . . .'

Very much the *grand seigneur* (and possibly one of the models for Proust's arrogant Baron de Charlus), Custine lived openly in a *ménage à trois* with two other men. One of his lovers was Edward Sainte-Barbe, a penniless Englishman, and the other Ignatius Gurowsky, a dashing and equally penniless young Pole who eventually married a Spanish infanta, one of Louis XIV's descendants. (Prosper Mérimée, the author of the novella on which *Carmen* was based, wrote to the mother of the future Empress Eugénie, 'Is it not a fine end to Louis XIV's line that one of his great-nieces should marry a Pole supported by a man?')

Custine was as celebrated for his way of life as for his writing. The author Barbey d'Aurevilly referred to Custine as 'the most voluptuous literary temperament and *the most sensitive mind* of his time'. Baudelaire wrote that Custine 'was a genius whose dandyism went so far as to encompass the ideal of negligence. Such gentlemanly good faith, such romantic ardour, such true irony, so absolute and nonchalant a personality, are inaccessible to the understanding of the common herd, and this precious writer had all the ill-fortune his talent deserved stacked against him.' How one responds to such a characterization, with all its landmine adjectives and quirky paradoxes, determines how far one has oneself roamed beyond the herd.

Homosexuality may have been looked at askance in nineteenth-century France (Custine was severely beaten up by a group of cavalry officers when he attempted to seduce one of their comrades), but the French-speaking world seems not to have been as pitiless and hysterical as the England that judged Oscar Wilde. The Irish wit was condemned to prison for homosexuality and released only after time spent doing hard labour, running on a giant treadmill and being forced to sleep on bare planks. The governor of the prison remarked when Wilde was released in 1897, 'He looks well. But like all men unused to manual labour who receive a sentence of this kind, he will be dead within two years.'

It took three years for Wilde to die, but the prediction was largely accurate. The broken man found refuge in Paris, where he'd lived in the

1880s at the height of his glory. Now, two decades later, he died on the block-long rue des Beaux-Arts in a little hotel, then known as the Hôtel d'Alsace, which now has been done up and renamed with chic understatement L'Hôtel. At the turn of the century it was so tawdry that shortly before he died Wilde declared to a woman friend, 'My wallpaper and I are fighting a duel to the death. One or the other of us has to go.'

Compared to Wilde's ignominious end, a French-speaking Belgian writer, Georges Eekhoud, got off lightly. Eekhoud wrote one of the first gay male novels in any language, *Escal Vigor*, and was charged by a Flemish court with pornography in 1900. Nearly every important French-speaking writer of the day, including André Gide, testified on his behalf – and Eekhoud was exonerated. Subsequently he even became a professor of literature at the Belgian Royal Academy.

When Wilde died on 30 November 1900 at the age of forty-two, he was buried in a humble grave in the suburb of Bagneux; only in 1909 were his remains moved to a more suitable tomb at Père Lachaise, where he was interred under a white winged angel carved by Sir Jacob Epstein (the angel looks vaguely Abyssinian). The inscription is a citation from *The Ballad of Reading Gaol*:

And alien tears will fill for him
Pity's long-broken urn,
For his mourners will be outcast men,
And outcasts always mourn.

In the 1920s gay Paris became more and more conspicuous. On the rue de Lappe, near the Bastille, and on the rue de Montagne St Geneviève, near the Panthéon, large gay balls were frequently given. On Mardi Gras and halfway through Lent, 'Magic City' balls were held on the rue Cognacq-Jay, and huge crowds of gawking straights gathered outside to watch the entrances made by drag queens and kings. But these balls were only the most visible manifestation of a gay life that had become highly organized since the turn of the century. Bars, nightclubs and saunas all catered to a public with 'special tastes'.

Despite France's tradition of tolerance, the collaborationist Vichy government set up by the Nazis tried to make things uncomfortable for homosexuals – but legally, at least, all it could change was the age of consent, which was raised to twenty-one. General de Gaulle himself perpetrated this invidious distinction: heterosexual activity was legal after age fifteen, whereas twenty-one remained the legal age for gay men.

This new puritanism ended only in 1981, when

the socialist government of François Mitterrand was voted overwhelmingly into power. The socialists had avidly courted the gay vote during the campaign and now the new government paid off its political debts handsomely. Mitterrand's Minister of the Interior, Gaston Defferre, instructed the police throughout the country no longer to specify the sexual orientation of people arrested, nor to discriminate in any way against homosexuals or homosexual establishments. The special 'homosexual brigade' of the police force was dissolved. There were to be no more raids on gay bars nor on gay cruising spots.

At the same time the President freed 150 prisoners who had been arrested for 'homosexual crimes'. A new housing law removed the words 'good fathers of families' with regard to desirable renters of houses or apartments. Other laws discriminatory against gays were dropped. Conversely, the legal definition of rape was now extended to protect both men and women against penetrative sexual acts in which force was used. Finally, a leftist majority lowered the legal age of consent to eighteen for homosexuals (some time earlier it had been raised from fifteen to eighteen for heterosexuals).

I can remember the heady days of 1981, when I paid a long visit to friends in Paris. When I moved to France in 1983 the euphoria was still in the air. I'd been conditioned by three decades of gay life in America to be in a permanent state of alert about possible police raids of bars, baths and cruising places; equally feared were roving gangs of queer-bashers. But in Paris the streets and parks and saunas and back rooms seemed positively tranquil by contrast.

Socially, gays were treated differently as well. In New York, at least in the 1960s and 70s, gays seldom ventured to gatherings out of the ghetto, whereas in Paris my American lover and I were invited everywhere and received as a couple, even if sometimes we were the only gay males present. In New York liberal straights would have found a way to reassure us that we were really, truly welcome, whereas in Paris (at least among the well-heeled, sophisticated, arty people we were meeting) no one ever mentioned our sexuality. Or if someone did it was in a general spirit of ribaldry, which so often presided over those worldly, lighthearted conversations.

In America gays had forged a new identity for themselves, one that had political clout, especially when AIDS became the dominant problem facing the community. But in France the entire government seemed to be pro-gay, which had stolen the thunder of gay activists. Indeed, when AIDS hit France full-force in 1985 (995 cases were recorded by the end of the year), the gay community scarcely existed and was ill-equipped to struggle against the disease. A reluctance to deal with the disease openly and honestly beset the country. The minister of health refused to receive the first and most important AIDS organization, AIDES. Typically, when the great philosopher Michel Foucault died of AIDS in 1984, the left-wing newspaper *Libération* had denied the real cause of death on the front page as though it were a calumny invented by his enemies.

France has had three times more known cases of AIDS than Britain since the very beginning of the epidemic. As of 30 June 1995, France had a cumulative count of 37,000 cases (including 17,200 homosexuals or bisexuals) and Great Britain had 11,051 cases (including 7,923 homo- or bisexuals). Since the two countries were hit by the virus at roughly the same time, have about the same size population, and each has a huge capital city where most of the gay population is concentrated, one would not have expected such skewed statistics.

The 6,000-case difference in the gay-bi populations of the two countries, which has only grown larger in subsequent years, begs for an explanation. Many theories spring to mind. For instance, France was one of the last countries in Europe to have an organized AIDS movement directed at gays. The Netherlands, Britain and Luxembourg had gay-run and gay-targeted AIDS associations by 1982, Germany and Spain by 1983, Denmark and Italy by 1984 – but Belgium and France inaugurated their organized struggle only in 1985.

Or one could argue that since Mitterrand's policies had led to the dissolution of gay activism, there were few gay leaders around when AIDS hit France. The arrival of AIDS and the demise of gay activism occurred at about the same time. Eventually new leaders emerged, but only with the advent of Act Up in the early 1990s.

Some historians of the phenomenon have tried to blame the far right in France or the power of the Catholic Church, but in fact both organisms formulated their anti-gay policies only in 1987– too late to be a significant factor. A better target is Mitterrand's extreme reticence (similar to Reagan's) even to mention the disease, much less to implement useful prevention programmes. For if France has always been strong in AIDS research and treatment, it has been very weak in prevention.

Part of the blame, surprisingly, can be attributed to French gay intellectuals and artists themselves; at least their attitudes are consistent with the response of the more general population. As early as 1982 Michel Foucault, writing under a pseudonym in *Libération*, declared that fear over 'gay cancer' in the United States had regrettably caused the American gay press and gay movement leaders to spread slogans 'in favour of monogamy and the couple and on the need to practise sports rather than sex'. As late as 1985 a journalist in the leading French gay periodical *Gai Pied* was declaring that AIDS is 'a sickness of the press' – a psychosis invented by sensationalists rather than a genuine problem. In the same year the famous gay militant and novelist Guy Hocquenhem wrote (also in *Gai Pied*): 'Tobacco causes cancer, we all know that. Have we stopped smoking? Sex causes diseases, should we stop making love? . . . How can we believe in a medical science that discourages us, which announces nothing but catastrophes of contagion, which keeps company only with fear and despair?' (The tragic irony is that both Foucault and Hocquenhem died of AIDS.)

The extreme reluctance of the French to recognize the gravity of AIDS or to campaign against its spread is linked to other national ambiguities that show up in an overview of French attitudes towards gays and literature in particular, and towards identity politics in general. For example, one of the great paradoxes is that France – the country that produced some of the most re-nowned pioneer homosexual writers of this cen-tury (Marcel Proust, André Gide, Jean Genet, Jean Cocteau and Marguerite Yourcenar, just to begin the list) – is also today the country that most vigorously rejects the very idea of gay literature. As Didier Eribon, the author of a major biography of Michel Foucault, pointed out, this response is all of a piece with a more general rejection in France of everything that smacks of a politics based on minorities or the legitimization of feminism.

The French constantly ridicule American-style university departments of women's studies or books or courses in the States on African Amer-ican or Jewish or Native American literature. The alarmist book *Une Amérique qui fait peur* (by Edward Behr) attributes most of America's ills to feminism. At the end of the 1980s the French expressed a general alarm about the excesses of political correctness in America and only the celebrated historian François Furet had the wit to point out to his compatriots that the excesses of racism and religious bigotry in the United States far outweigh the dangers of political correctness – which in any event holds sway only on liberal campuses.

Perhaps the most telling contrast between France and the English-speaking world, however, is over the whole question of lesbian and gay literature. In all of France there is only one big gay bookstore, Les Mots à la bouche, which is in Paris. And in the 1990s there was not one serious, literary, nonpornographic gay publication, due to a lack of advertising support. When I was interviewed by the (now defunct) French gay literary magazine *Masques* in the early 1980s, I was asked if I considered myself a 'gay writer'. When I said 'Of course', the astonished journalist told me I was the first person the magazine had ever interviewed who'd said yes to that question. When an international gay literary conference was held in London in the mid-1980s, several French writers were invited but only one lesbian accepted; all the others indignantly refused.

This attitude among gay French writers and thinkers seems weirdly at odds with the startling fact that AIDS was the cause of more than half of all deaths in 1987 of French men in the media, the arts and entertainment.

Or take another example: when Frédéric

Martel's history of the modern French gay movement, *Le Rose et le noir*, was published, the promotional pamphlet announced, 'Not at all a history of a "minority" or of a "community" – debatable terms – but rather a skein of individual paths that end up by composing what could be called a "group with a destiny".

American or British or German gays often dismiss the French as simply being 'closeted' – fearful, Catholic, guilt-ridden, conformist. But the curious thing is that the very writers in France who would most strenuously reject the label of 'gay writer' are often those who have been the most explicit and courageous in the presentation of their homosexuality. In 1972 Hocquenhem published in *Le Nouvel Observateur* an article titled 'The Revolution of Homosexuals'. In 1979 Renaud Camus published *Tricks*, a blow-by-blow account, as it were, of his gay sexual adventures. Tony Duvert in *When Jonathan Died* spoke with startling frankness about one of *the* great taboo subjects, man – boy love. And Yves Navarre (who committed suicide in 1994) wrote in *Our Share of Time* about a forty-year-old schoolteacher's love for a much younger man. Yet no gay male writer, with perhaps the sole exception of Guillaume Dustan, would accept the 'gay writer' label. Typically, the gay writer Dominique Fernandez has argued that the degree of acceptance that gays won in the 1970s had a disastrous, lowering effect on their writing which only the new stigmatization brought about by AIDS might correct. And in any event Fernandez does not want to be 'reduced' to a label. And Roland Barthes – one of the handful of postwar French writers to win an international reputation – never 'came out' in print. The most he could say, as James Creech has pointed out, was that *perversion* 'produces a *plus*: I am more sensitive, more perceptive, more loquacious, better entertained, etc., and in this *plus*, difference comes to take up residence (and thus, the Text of life, life as text) . . .'

A cynic might argue that French writers who reject the 'gay' label have been able to stay sufficiently in the mainstream to win lots of honours. Hector Bianciotti may have written about his gay experiences in a seminary, but he is still sufficiently discreet to have been elected a member of the French Academy in 1995. Fernandez won the Prix Médicis in 1974 and the Goncourt in 1982; Yves Navarre won the Goncourt in 1980 and quickly thereafter seemed to become *the* 'homosexual writer' in France – although, of course, he angrily rejected this designation and published a book about his cat.

What is certain is that these elusive writers have been able to keep a general readership, sell lots of copies and win prizes with their fiction, whereas no clearly labelled gay writer in America or Britain has ever enjoyed a comparable renown or popularity.

The French themselves would argue that their rejection of all ghettoization, far from being a sign of closetedness or cynicism, is in fact consistent with their 'singularity' as a nation. The French believe that a society is not a federation of special interest groups but rather an impartial state that treats each citizen – regardless of his or her gender, sexual orientation, religion or colour – as an abstract, universal individual. For the French any subgroup of citizens is a *diminishment* of human equality. This is a position stated with eloquence and clarity by Mona Ozouf in her book *The Words of Women: An Essay on French Singularity*. Or as the social commentator Michael Pollak has put it, 'In France specific groups linked together by a shared identity are generally perceived as illegitimate.'

The only problem is that this universality and impartiality don't always defend the rights of particular groups. As Ozouf points out, France is the country where women in Europe have the highest level of education. Already in 1963, for instance, 43 per cent of French students were women, as opposed to 32 per cent in England and 24 per cent in West Germany. But this academic equality has not been matched with power in the society at large. French women gained the right to vote only after the Second World War – *after* women in India and Turkey. And even today in France there is a smaller percentage of women in high government posts or in executive positions in business than in any other European country, including Portugal.

This inequality is rapidly changing, fortunately. For instance, in 1999 Jospin's government passed the law of *parité* which penalized political parties that failed to offer voters a slate at the polls that was not equally balanced between male and female candidates. And the PACS law has won marital rights for gay and lesbian couples – or for any two people living under the same roof for more than three years.

Despite these gains, the lack of community organization among French gays and the lack of political representation have meant that France has been particularly hard hit by AIDS and has responded slowly and late to the crisis.

The problem is that the leading French AIDS organization, AIDES, felt that given the national character, it could not address itself directly to gays. Daniel Defert, Foucault's surviving partner and the power behind AIDES, recently said:

> In 1984, with 294 known cases in France, there weren't very many activists and those who were ill and mobilized were mostly homosexual. Those who were ill thought that to publicize their AIDS would be a real burden, just as to announce their homosexuality publicly would have been difficult since most of them had not discussed it with the people around them.

When Defert showed the ill members of his organization a poster clearly aimed at the gay community, they rejected it: 'They wanted their image to be respected at the hospital.' As Frédéric Martel puts it, 'What is the best way to fight an epidemic: the American-style identity-politics model and multiculturalism or the (French-style) universalist – or even republican – model?'

The first AIDS campaign in France, launched only in 1987, rallied behind the vague slogan 'AIDS won't be passed along by me'. In the same year a splinter group, AFLS, began to use more militant tactics to reach gays more directly, but by then the numbers affected were already appalling and a fatalistic mood had set in among

French homosexuals. Act Up – which held its first meeting on 12 July 1989 – was a significant and courageous rejection of everything typically French. It was strident and confrontational, and it noisily took its stand as a specifically gay organization made up of many members who were themselves HIV-positive, whereas AIDES had never advertised the sexual orientation nor the health status of its member. In fact Didier Lestrade, the openly gay and HIV-positive founder of Act Up in France, has admitted that he instinctively rejected Michel Foucault's writing from the outset:

> Act Up arrived at the very moment when denial of homosexuality had reached its extreme limit. Suddenly I decided early on that in order to be the president of Act Up I would have to forego reading Foucault. Not that I felt a cultural inferiority complex, but Foucault's thinking had so marked the first organizations in the struggle against AIDS that I had to save myself from its influence.

The French way of looking at homosexuality – or any other special-interest group – *is* defensible. Characteristically, the French think that sexuality is a private matter that should not be politicized or even discussed. This discretion, joined to a secularism that approaches atheism, has meant that French gays have not come in for any of the fag-bashing they've had to endure in the States at the hands of rednecks, fascists and Christian fundamentalists. But French individualism – abstract and universal – along with a corresponding scorn of identity politics, has made France unusually vulnerable to AIDS.

Finally, the paradox of the French spirit, which is boldly outspoken about individual experience but against all communitarianism based on that experience, is best reflected in its literature. France has given the Goncourt Prize to the Haitian writer Patrick Chamoiseau – but there is no 'black novel' in France. Similarly, the movie actress Simone Signoret could publish a novel about Jews in the Second World War – but there is no 'Jewish novel' in France. And, most dramatically, so many of the leading French writers of the twentieth century have written openly about their homosexuality – but the label 'gay fiction' evokes only a tired smile in Paris.

CHAPTER SIX

THE *FLÂNEUR* IN SEARCH of the Paris past, including the past of French kings and queens, never has far to go. Generations of royalty are buried at the Basilique de Saint Denis, which is the next-to-last stop on one of the métro lines, to the north of the city. The first known member of a royal family to be buried there was Arégonde, the second wife of Clotaire I – she was interred towards the end of the sixth century. Named after the first bishop of Paris (the martyr Denis, who was killed in 250 for trying to convert the pagan French), the basilica was the burial place of such early kings as Charles Martel, the hero who drove back the Muslim invasion (he died in 741), and Pépin le Bref (dead in 768), the father of Charlemagne. But it became a royal necropolis only under the Capetian dynasty. Hugues Capet

Edmund White

died in 996, and from then until the end of the
Bourbon dynasty in the eighteenth century, every
French king was buried here. In addition, the
sceptre, crown and sword were housed here, and
many of the queens of France were crowned here
(whereas the kings were crowned at Rheims).

The church became a cathedral in 1966; before
that it was a royal abbey, often ruled by kings
who served as abbots. Although St Denis attracts
visitors because it was one of the first Gothic
churches in France and because it still has some
of its original twelfth-century stained-glass windows, nevertheless its main draw is as the burial
place of kings and queens. For French *royalists*, it
is indeed one of the most sacred places anywhere.
Here they can pray before the Renaissance tomb
of Catherine de Médicis and Henri II and the
statues of the king and queen martyred by the
Revolution, Louis XVI and Marie Antoinette.
(Curiously, the sculptor has made Marie Antoinette appear almost sluttish in her extremely dé-
colleté gown; with one hand she invitingly cups
her very full breast!)

Of course Louis XVI and his Austrian-born
wife were not buried here with the usual Bourbon
pomp after they were beheaded. Louis XVI was
executed on 21 January 1793, after a two-month-
long trial; his sentence of death was decided by just

one vote – 361 delegates against 360. The queen was guillotined nine months later by the son of her husband's headsman. For the royal executions, what is now known as the Place de la Concorde (and what had originally been called Place Louis XV) was rebaptized the Place de la Révolution. On 21 January 1993 some five thousand monarchists gathered in the Place de la Concorde at exactly 10.22 a.m. to the minute to mark the two-hundredth anniversary of the king's decapitation. The American ambassador in 1993, Walter Curley, himself an expert on kings and queens, laid a bouquet on the square in memory of Louis XVI's support of the American Revolution. Some modern-day Jacobins showed up to ridicule the royalists – and bore aloft a calf's head.

This square, oddly enough, had been the scene of an earlier tragedy, on 30 May 1770, at the time of Marie Antoinette's marriage to the king. Some fireworks, intended to dazzle the public, had caught fire, burned the temporary temple to Hymen, and killed dozens of bystanders. Still more suffocated in the stampede of the frightened crowd; their bodies were buried at the cemetery of the Madeleine, just north of the Place. Some twenty-three years later the bodies of the royal couple would be tossed into a common grave in the same cemetery.

There they lay until the restoration of the royal
family in 1815, even though in the meanwhile
Napoleon had already considered rehabilitating
their names and honouring their remains. When
he was building the Madeleine he said, 'Do you
really think I want to build a temple to glory?'
(There had been some talk of turning the site into
a secular temple to the memory of French soldiers
fallen in battle.) 'No, I want a church and in this
church there will be an expiatory chapel where
the remains of Louis XVI and Marie Antoinette
will be deposed, but that will take time thanks to
these bastards who surround me.' In fact Napoleon never had the time necessary to make this
conciliatory gesture.

In 1815, after Napoleon was defeated the
second time and a Bourbon, Louis XVIII, was
placed on the throne, two men (the grandson of
the gravedigger and a royalist magistrate whose
windows looked down on the cemetery) indicated where the king and queen had been buried.
Their remains were exhumed on 21 January, the
anniversary of the king's death, and transferred
to the crypt beneath the altar at the basilica of St
Denis. A year later Louis XVI's daughter, the
Duchesse d'Angoulême, convinced the new king
to order a commemorative edifice. Work began
on the 'expiatory chapel' to mark the place where

the bodies had lain for so many years; it was not completed until a decade later, in 1826.

This chapel, built to resemble a Graeco-Roman tomb, is sufficiently melancholy to fascinate the *flâneur*. On the corner of the Boulevard Haussmann and the rue Pasquier, the chapel is just six or seven blocks behind the Place de la Concorde and a stone's throw from the Gare St Lazare. Proust could look down on it from his apartment at 102 Boulevard Haussmann. Did having it constantly in view make him even more acutely aware of the transitoriness of worldly glory? It's in a noisy, busy office district, but the chapel and its grounds form an island of tranquillity, a forgotten corner in a neighbourhood of department stores and cheap hotels for the travelling salesmen and travellers on a budget who arrive every day at the Gare St Lazare.

The chapel is open only on Thursdays, Fridays and Saturdays – and then only in the afternoon. The entrance fee is fifteen francs. Large stone tombs, the final resting place for the members of the Swiss Guardsmen who were killed defending Louis XVI, line the pathway that leads up to an impressive pale stone Neo-Classical porch with pillars, the whole building cupped under a light-green dome pierced by a single window, like the

Pantheon in Rome. Inside and to the right is a statue of Louis XVI kneeling in fleur-de-lys robes and supported by an angel (a teenage boy) standing on tiptoe. Below the statue is a black stone with the king's final testament engraved in gold letters. On the other side of the spacious, high-ceilinged room is a matching statue of Marie Antoinette with her son, the dauphin. Below her is her last letter to her sister, in which she forgives her enemies and confesses she is dying in her faith, convinced of her innocence. Over the entrance door is a marble bas-relief picturing a procession, the king's burial – or is it the 1815 reburial? On the far wall, under a half-dome, is an austere altar; downstairs yet another altar is placed in a low-roofed crypt.

Outside there are benches under hundred-year-old trees, children playing, pensioners sitting in solitude while all around them swarms the slightly muffled life of the polluted city. Across the street are the display windows of a traditional maker of artificial flowers. I wonder if the idea of this royal chapel for expiating the sins of the nation against its king and queen might have inspired the building of Sacré-Coeur in Montmartre, which was begun in 1875 by the Third Republic to expiate the excesses of the Commune of 1871 – a desperate, anarchic movement that had claimed Montmartre itself as its last, bloody stronghold.

I've met few royalists other than my eighty-five-year-old landlady, a starchy *grande dame* who corrected me and said she was not a royalist but a monarchist, a distinction that even after consulting my dictionary I couldn't quite grasp. 'After all, Monsieur White, just look at what two centuries of the Republic has brought us – it's rather sad, *n'est-ce pas?*' She lowered her head in a display of regret and smug certainty. She is an admirable woman who works without pay for the Doctors Without Borders, and her son – another convinced monarchist – served as a doctor for free in Kosovo for a month.

She was very opposed to the American bombing of the Serbs – 'who, after all, were our *allies* during the war of 1914–18 . . .' (what's implied is that they are Christians and not Muslims). She is anti-American, partly because of disgraceful shenanigans in the White House but mainly because she is opposed to the American domination of European politics, economy and culture.

Madame is a descendant of a famous French family of the far right, but she is careful to side-step controversy in conversation, though she admits that she disapproves of any additional immigrants being admitted into France. 'France always welcomed unfortunate people,' she says softly but firmly, 'but now we can't do anything more.' She reads *Action Française*, a right-wing weekly paper that calls for a return to the monarchy.

A much younger friend of mine, an artist in her forties, told me that she had grown up with the daughter of a celebrated if reactionary writer. Their paths had separated for years when my friend had moved with her parents to the Caribbean. The conservative writer's daughter, in the meanwhile, had married an aristocrat and picked up all his still more conservative views, including rabid anti-Semitism. She's now convinced the world is ruled by an international Jewish conspiracy. When the two girlhood friends recently arranged for a reunion in Paris after not seeing each other for two decades, the writer's daughter (who is now a duchess) unveiled her conspiracy theory. Her old friend, the artist, was so appalled she burst into tears. The duchess, of course, is a convinced monarchist, although to be sure in Paris there is even room for *socialist* monarchists as well – an even odder and wholly unpredictable ultimate development of the French Revolution.

Most French royalist aspirations were placed for decades in the Count of Paris, Henri d'Orléans, who endorsed the socialist candidate François Mitterrand when he was running in 1988 for his second term as President. The Count had been born and raised in Morocco, since during his youth the royal family was not permitted to live in France. He then became a student in Brussels, where he took up medicine, the law and agriculture, a bit of everything to prepare for his royal role. Henri, unexpectedly, rejected the fascist views of the Action Française, and earned the enmity of its leader Charles Maurras. One of the chief conflicts in the royalist camp is that the various pretenders to the throne are all fairly progressive politically, whereas the Action Française and the other far-right groups that support them are all quite reactionary.

In 1931 the Count of Paris married his cousin Isabelle, Princess of Orléans and Bragance. The wedding took place in Palermo, Sicily, since the French government feared the political repercussions of a ceremony if it were held nearer France, in Belgium. In rapid succession Isabelle was to give him eleven children. In 1940 Henri was allowed to join the French Foreign Legion under the pseudonym of Robert Orliac. In 1950 the French parliament voted to overturn the law, established in 1886, which had forbidden the heirs of former rulers to live in France. Now

the Count of Paris and his wife Isabelle returned
to France with their eleven children.

The Count – or Prince, as his followers called
him – visited each region of France for a few days
and, predictably, discovered 'an unchanging
France that jealously preserves its virtues and
hopes'. The family lived in enormous luxury
and the children's marriages were celebrated with
quasi-royal pomp. The Count received leaders of
each political party in an effort to show he was
statesmanlike and above all factions. He hoped
de Gaulle would name him his successor, but de
Gaulle merely asked, with some asperity, why
not, in that case, 'the Queen of the Gypsies?'

As the years flew by, the great question became, who would succeed the ageing Count as
the head of the house of France and heir to the
throne? The Count hesitated between his son and
grandson, until in 1987 – during a celebration of
the thousand years of existence of the French
monarchy, or at least of the Capetian dynasty –
he named his grandson Jean his heir. Before an
audience of some three thousand people he invested Jean as the duc de Vendôme. Henri's wife,
the Countess Isabelle, had meanwhile demanded
a separation – and the Count moved to another
house with a mistress, Monique Friez. For the
rest of his life he would see Isabelle only during

official occasions. At last, in 1996, the Count had a reconciliation with his son Henri, the Count de Clermont, even though he disapproved of the younger Henri's divorce from his wife and of his sole real passion – painting.

The Count of Paris had inherited in 1940 the equivalent of $200 million in today's money. In 1999, when he died, he left nothing to his children. In fact nothing could be found of his vast fortune – nothing but six monogrammed handkerchiefs. Starting in 1975, the year he'd met his mistress, the Count had begun to sell off all his holdings at such a rapid rate that the Countess and her children had taken out an injunction to stop one particular auction at Sotheby's. They succeeded, but only temporarily. The Count had inherited not only money and a bulging stock portfolio but also extensive lands, two sapphire and diamond tiaras, childhood drawings done by Louis XIV, a portrait of Louis XIII by Philippe de Champaigne and countless other treasures. He was caught trying to sneak one of his tiaras out of France and into Switzerland and was forced to sell it to the Louvre for a mere $1 million. He began to sell off the family's estates in Morocco, Portugal, Sicily and France at a dizzying rate. Over a twenty-year period he sold all his works of art for some $5 million.

His mistress nursed him through a serious bout with cancer, but in return asked to become the administrator of his private foundation, which consumed his fortune at an even brisker pace. Towards the end of his life, when the Count was interviewed, he expressed his disdain for his family. His wife? 'I've never had much of anything to say to her.' The family? 'A secondary event.' His sons and daughters? 'They've disappointed me. They won't inherit anything.'

True to his word, he left them nothing but the six monogrammed handkerchiefs, a pair of slippers and a forest in the former duchy of Guise. It was an anticlimactic ending to the dazzling build-up of an unexpectedly brilliant name and fortune. Henri had sworn that he would be the last of the Capetians.

The Count of Paris was an Orleanist – that is, a descendant of Philippe l'Egalité, the Duc d'Orléans who voted to behead Louis XVI, his cousin, and was in turn beheaded by the Jacobins a year later. At the time of his vote to kill the king, Philippe was serving as a deputy from Paris to the Convention under the name of 'Equality'. His son later, after years of exile in England and America, became Louis-Philippe, French king from 1830 to 1848 – until the mob chased him once again into exile in England. Those Frenchmen today who remain faithful to the memory of the Bourbons fiercely reject the Orleanist claims to the throne.

I had an apartment between the Centre Georges Pompidou and the Tour St Jacques until 1998, when I moved back to the States. While I lived in that neighbourhood I often stopped at the corner café, the Bar-Tabac des Templiers at 35 rue de Rivoli, just a block from the Hôtel de Ville, the Town Hall of Paris. In some ways it was just a typical noisy big-city café with plastic-covered chairs, butts ground out on the tile floor, pinball machines, streaked plate-glass windows, a line of people in front of the window that sold cigarettes and stamps and lottery tickets. Most of the customers are taxi drivers, and two or three taxis are always parked out front.

But even the least observant visitor would notice strange details after a moment: a life-size statue of Joan of Arc in armour with a banner; small, mass-produced plaster busts of Louis XVI and Marie Antoinette inside a vitrine; on the door a big poster reprinting Louis XVI's last testament; on one wall a picture of the Bourbon (as opposed to the Orleanist) pretender – the very young and handsome Louis XX, as his followers call him, or the Duc d'Anjou, as he is referred to in his native Spain.

Louis XX (as the owner of the bar told me) may be Spanish, but in fact he is 'French-Spanish', and in the year 2000 he was just twenty-six years old. He was born on 25 April 1974 – 760 years to the day after the birth of his ancestor St Louis. He is tall, dark and handsome, permanently tanned, thick-lipped, with small ears and heavy lobes, a little, plumb-straight nose and eyebrows as thick as Brooke Shields's. His full title is Monseigneur le Prince Louis, duc d'Anjou et de Bourbon: head of the house of Bourbon. Among his ancestors he counts eight saints (St Louis is only the best-known), which for their loyal admirers places the living members of the family in a direct tradition of all that is most holy in France. Prince Louis became the Bourbon heir only after the death of his older brother in a car accident in 1984 and of his father in a ghastly skiing accident on 30 January 1989.

Here the owner of the Bar-Tabac des Templiers becomes excited and leans towards me. 'He died – and it was a Republican conspiracy. He was skiing down a slope in Colorado and someone – I think we know who – put an invisible wire across the path that sliced off his head – exactly on the centennial of the Revolution.' (I could picture the headline: 'Regicide at Beaver Creek'.)

When I asked the owner why he had such respect for the royal family, he said, 'Well, the Bourbons are descended from Jesus through St Anne, the kings of Troy and eventually Clovis, the Capetians and all the Louis.' When I called him a monarchist, he corrected me and said, 'I'm a royalist, not a monarchist', though I have yet to grasp the difference. He informed me that there are some 75,000 royalists in Paris alone and that that very evening there would be an exciting meeting at the bar of half a dozen young royalists.

When I asked him about the allegorical paintings at the back of the bar, he said they were by a South American and showed the three paths as well as the jungle, the desert and the three wise men. My head began to swim when he told me the paintings showed the 'inequality underlying all life'.

'What is your idea of an ideal government?' I asked.

'I long for a government of lords. No more politicians. The lords won't be paid, since they're already rich – so there will be no more corruption. Above them will be the king, of course.' He handed me a printed sheet calling for the end of the Republic, which had established greed as the ultimate value, and a return to the monarchy. In his programme was a rejection of a one-world government in favour of smaller territories that remained true to their racial heritage and their religion. Interestingly in secular France, the pamphleteer had added:

> Even without being believers we should recognize the practical and moral values of religion: control of the powerful, sociological unity of an ethnic group, the idealism of a personal journey for each person instructed by his own religion and, finally, the 'psychotherapy' due to following a religion that restores the harmony between an unconscious inherited from our ancestors and a daily life dictated by their very religion.

The current Bourbon heir to the throne has made several appearances in France to strengthen his claims. He never seems to miss a trick. For the millennium of Capetian rule he visited Rheims and was shown the vial of holy oil used to anoint the kings – a sort of preview of things to come and a good photo op. He also travelled to Versailles and was photographed in the Hall of Mirrors, and attended a Mass at Aigues-Mortes to celebrate the departure for the Holy Land of his namesake St Louis in 1248. Louis XX was present at St Denis for a Mass on 21 January 1993 in honour of Louis XVI, and he planted a tree in 1994 to commemorate the coronation of his ancestor Henri IV.

I stumbled out of the Bar-Tabac a bit stunned, carrying several pamphlets, my head stuffed with invectives against the Orleanists – 'Philippe l'Egalité swore to the Revolutionaries that he was not the son of the Duc d'Orléans but of a stableboy' – and solemn praise for the current Bourbon.

As I hurried off, I took one last look at the photo of Louis XX and thought I'd be willing to obey him – at least better him than anyone else, although the Queen of the Gypsies sounded like another viable option.

Flânerie is the best way to impose a personal vision on the palimpsest of Paris. It's a bit like being a film director who puts together his own take on a place by selecting only those scenes that conform to it – as if one were to show only the wild birds that live in the highest towers of Manhattan, thereby converting this most artificial of cities into something bucolic, or as if one were to concentrate only on the industrial wasteland of Mestre across the bay from Venice, thus turning the most perfect Byzantine and Renaissance fairyland into the Detroit of Italy.

Paris is dominated by its classical monuments and the great sweeping perspectives between them, and this formal face is irresistible. It is a city that has been designed and preserved through the simplifying willpower of kings, emperors and autocratic presidents. No one could object to this official guise of the city, which looks so peaceful and eternal and natural that only a historian could remember how slowly it was put together – and how contested was each step of construction.

For instance, the vista that extends from I. M. Pei's pyramid at the Louvre to Napoleon's nearby Arc du Carrousel to the horses of Marly framing the Champs-Elysées down to the Arc du Triomphe and on to the distant Grande Arche looks as if one town planner had laid it out in a single moment of inspiration. But in fact it is bookended by Mitterrand's *grands projets* of the 1980s and holds in between them architectural ideas of the eighteenth and nineteenth centuries defended by the Bourbons and both Napoleons. At every point the slightest innovation has provoked endless debate; in the 1980s we used to say that the only difference between the left- and right-wingers in that prosperous and untroubled era was that the socialists liked the Pei pyramid and the conservatives detested it – on principle. No one ever seemed to have an unmediated or spontaneous aesthetic response to it. I surprised visiting Americans who asked me for my opinion. 'I like it,' I said with a deadpan expression. 'I'm a socialist.'

The shorter vista from the Madeleine to the Assemblée Nationale by way of the Place de la Concorde is silted with blood, forgotten ambitions and the cunning of art, but only historical X-ray eyes could ever see a substratum of so much conflict and emotion. And no one would ever guess, just by looking, that the rather sterile Île de la Cité, site of government buildings, the police headquarters and the sandblasted shell of Nôtre-Dame, was once a dangerous, malodorous rats' nest of the poor and of thieves and professional beggars, the fictional denizens of *Les Mystères de Paris* and *Les Misérables*, and that until the mid-nineteenth century rickety tenements crowded right up to the façade of the church. That grand esplanade, the Parvis, is a fairly recent innovation.

Nor would anyone ever imagine by just looking at the ghastly new opera house, which resembles a cow palace in Fort Worth, that the Place de la Bastille was once the site of a prison that the Revolution dismantled, even though it housed only a handful of inmates, including the Marquis de Sade, surely anyone's best candidate for incarceration. Rumour has it that Mitterrand chose an obscure Uruguyan living in Canada to build the new opera house by mistake: he had been told to pick out of the five models on display the one all the way to the left (Richard Meier's) but Mitterrand got confused and took the one all the way to the right (Carlos Ott's). If the Grande Arche and the Pei pyramid are Mitterrand's successes, then his outright failures must include not only the Bastille but also the new Bibliothèque Nationale, four glass buildings along the Seine designed to resemble four open books. As everyone knows, sunlight through glass is exactly what fragile rare books do not need; after the towers were put up, experts insisted that they be given an inner lining of opaque wood. The computerized book-retrieval system failed to function properly for so long the staff went on strike.

Despite a few glitches, Baron Haussmann's concept of a uniform Paris laid out along the most imperial lines has triumphed – a Paris that is efficient, clean, modern and always impressive. But in the cracks are those little forgotten places that appeal to the *flâneur*, the traces left by people living in the margin – Jews, blacks, gays, Arabs – or mementoes of an earlier, more chaotic and medieval France. Places like the Passage Brady where Indian wholesalers sit in turbaned splendour beside aromatic barrels of spices and trade in the latest videos of films from Bollywood. Or places like the Village St Paul, the collection of dozens of antique stores hidden in the oldest part of the Marais, close to the Seine. Or places like the Montmartre nightclub that on Sundays has its interracial all-male social evenings devoted to *Blancs, Blacks et Beurs*; that is, to whites and blacks and Arabs born and brought up in France. Or the sublime Sainte-Chapelle, the narrow church that the credulous king St Louis built to house a splinter of the True Cross (he also bought a drop of the Holy Mother's milk). The Sainte-Chapelle, secreted away behind a pompous nineteenth-century courthouse on the Île de la Cité, is one of the few places in Paris that convey a true piety, with its tall, exalted stained-glass windows casting colours on marble floors and its high gilt altar, where the king himself would expose his relics once a year to his adoring subjects (the servants worshipped in the low-roofed ground-floor chapel downstairs).

For me Paris lives in its details – the blue windows set in the doors of the boxes at the

Opéra Comique, the only (and magical) source of illumination during that moment just after the house lights are lowered and before the stage curtain is raised. The drama with which the waiters cluster around a table in a first-class restaurant and all lift the silver bell-shaped covers at the same moment to reveal the contents of the plates – and the pedantry with which one of the waiters explains in singsong detail exactly what each dish contains. The pleasant shock of the klieg lights that suddenly turn night into day when a *bâteau mouche* glides by. The melancholy mood (worthy of an old-fashioned production of *Pelléas et Mélisande*) of an autumn day when one rows over to one of the islands in the Grand Lac of the Bois de Boulogne in order to have lunch in a deserted restaurant – or the squalid excitement when one staggers through the bushes nearby at night to see the theatrical costumes and man-oeuvres of glamorous transvestite prostitutes from Brazil striking poses in the glare of passing headlights.

The *flâneur* knows where to find the best sashimi and the best couscous, but he is not just awash with *bonnes adresses*. Like a Balzacian hero he has seen all of Paris stretching out at his feet as he stands on the steps of that mortuary chapel to French military ambitions, the Sacré-

Coeur. He knows his way around the parks and marketplaces, the book stalls and the *grands magasins*; these are the world's first department stores, celebrated in Zola's novel *Le Bonheur des dames*, which ends with a massive white sale.

Christopher Isherwood once said that Berlin had become the capital of homosexual Europe in the 1920s because Paris had already cornered the much more lucrative heterosexual market, but the *flâneur* knows that this city accommodates all tastes, including the *flâneur*'s own for solitude in a crowd, for rustication in a hard-working metropolis, for collecting impressions in a marketplace devoted to the most varied and valuable sort of collections (everything from first editions to old prints, from *Art Nouveau* desks carved to resemble plants to the newest, grittiest art from the American ghetto). Inuit carvings, Tibetan weavings, African fetishes – there is every object to satisfy every appetite, including a few that are traditionally Gallic. But there are also these mental snapshots, these *instantanées* of fugitive life, these curving banisters and lacquered portals, these cold, empty quays beside the Seine where someone under a bridge is playing a saxophone – all the priceless but free memories only waiting for a *flâneur* to make them his own.

FURTHER READING

There is an embarrassment of riches when it comes to guidebooks about Paris. The books I found the most valuable included *Around and About Paris* by Thirza Vallois, arranged by arrondissements and published in four volumes, available in paperback from Iliad Books. Volume I came out in 1995. A one-volume but comprehensive guide is *Paris* from Hachette (1994), in French, with introductory chapters on the history of the city followed by an A to Z of sites. It is part of Le Guide du Patrimoine series edited by Jean-Marie Pérouse de Montclos.

The Time Out guides to Paris are yearly listings and evaluations of hotels and restaurants with sightseeing chapters thrown in and many mini-essays ('Impressionist Paris', 'The Jazz Age', etc.).

A good essay on multicultural Paris is Juan

Goytisolo's 'Paris, Capital of the Twenty-First Century' in his *The Forest of Literature* (El Bosque de las letras).

More specialized is the *Guide du Paris Savant* by Anna Alter and Philippe Testard-Vaillant (Belin, 1997), devoted to entries about everything of scientific interest in Paris, including museums of natural history, zoos, research centres and all the statues in town commemorating scientific leaders. *Paris: A Literary Companion* by Ian Littlewood (Harper & Row, 1988, also available as a Perennial paperback) is a fast, amusing read, which gives anecdotes about writers classed by the districts in which they lived. *Le Paris des étrangers*, essays edited by Kaspi and Marès (Imprimerie National, 1989), is a wide-angled look at the adventures of foreigners in Paris in the twentieth century.

Connaissance du Vieux Paris by Jacques Hillairet (Rivages, 1993, a reissue of a text of the 1950s) is a nearly-700-page tome full of historical anecdotes. Hillairet also wrote the wonderful two-volume *Dictionnaire historique des rues de Paris* (two volumes, Editions de Minuit, 1985).

Paris secret et insolite by Rodolphe Trouilleux (Parigramme, 1996) is a guide to the hidden, often unknown corners of the city. *Histoire et dictionnaire de Paris* by Alfred Pierro (Bouquins,

1996) is some 1,500 pages on the historical background of Paris. *Paris: Deux mille ans d'histoire* by Jean Favier (Fayard, 1997) is a thousand-page opus full of excellent summaries.

There are many series, casual or scholarly, that devote a volume to each arrondissement; Editions Hervas publishes a collection that I referred to. John Russell, the *New York Times* art critic and a very graceful writer, has published a splendid, heavily illustrated *Paris* (Abrams, updated in 1983).

Balzac's best portrait of Parisians comes from the opening pages of *The Girl with the Golden Eyes* (I quote from Carol Cosman's translation, published by Carroll & Graf, New York, 1998). I quote from Robert McAlmon's *Being Geniuses Together, 1920–1930*, revised with supplementary chapters and an afterword by Kay Boyle (Johns Hopkins, 1968, reissued as a paperback 1997). This is a gossipy book about the American lost generation in Paris in the 1920s. In her *Paris Notebooks* (Bloomsbury, 1988) the eloquent Mavis Gallant gives a selection of her nonfiction writing, including extraordinary essays on May 1968 and the French legal system. I consulted Strindberg's *Inferno* (Hutchinson, 1962), his account of his years in Paris in the 1890s, which was written in

Edmund White

French. For my epigraph and for other information I read *Memoirs of Montparnasse* by
John Glassco (Oxford, 1995), first published
in 1970 by a Canadian recalling his expatriate
life in Paris beginning in 1928. *Four Lives in
Paris* by Hugh Ford (North Point, 1987) gives
crucial portraits of the 1920s and 30s. Herbert
R. Lottman's *The Left Bank* (Chicago, 1982)
recounts the life of St Germain from the 1930s
through to the Cold War and gives a good
background to the importance of Simone de
Beauvoir and Jean-Paul Sartre.

The best books on Colette are her own, though
they are highly unreliable. Judith Thurman has
written the definitive biography, *Secrets of the
Flesh: A Life of Colette*, published in 1999 by
Bloomsbury and by Knopf. There is also a recent
two-volume biography by Claude Francis and
Fernande Gontier, called *Creating Colette*, published by Steerforth, which discusses Colette's
black ancestry in fascinating detail.

Tales of the New Babylon by Rupert Chris-
tiansen (Sinclair-Stevenson) has an excellent
chapter on Baron Haussmann. *The Painting of
Modern Life: Paris in the Art of Manet and His
Followers* by T. J. Clark (Princeton, 1984) is also
absorbing in its discussion of the rebuilding of
Paris in the nineteenth century. *Les Ecrivains*

devant l'Impressionnisme, edited by Denys Riout (Macula, 1989), gives a clear picture of the aesthetic climate of the 1870s and 80s.

In writing about the *flâneur* I read the catalogue for the Musée Carnavalet's exhibition *Les Rues de Paris au XVIII siècle: le regard de Louis Sébastien Mercier* by Elizabeth Bourginat (1999). I relied heavily on the classic text by Baudelaire, *Le Peintre de la vie moderne* (reprinted in the second volume of the *Oeuvres complètes* published by the Pléiade, but available in many languages and editions). For this discussion I also looked at Walter Benjamin's *Paris: Capitale du XIX siècle: le livre des passages* (Cerf, 1989), which of course exists in German and was recently translated into English as *The Arcades Project* (Belknap/Harvard, 1999). I also read Benjamin's 'The Return of the Flâneur' in *Selected Writings*, vol. 2 (Belknap/Harvard, 1999). Sylviane Agacinski said many interesting things about the *flâneur* in *Le Passeur de Temps* (Seuil, 2000).

I quoted from André Breton's *L'Amour fou*, which I read in the second volume of the Pléiade edition, 1992. I also read Breton's *Nadja* in English (Grove, 1960). I also studied *The World of Atget* by Berenice Abbott (Paragon, 1964).

In writing about African Americans in Paris, I consulted Tyler Stovall's *African-Americans in the City of Light* (Houghton Mifflin, 1996) and *From Harlem to Paris: Black American Writers in France, 1840–1980* by Michel Fabre (University of Illinois, 1993). *A Street Guide to African Americans in Paris* by Michel Fabre and John A. Williams (Cercle d'études Afro-Américaines, 1996) discusses in vivid detail the lives and locations of many celebrated women and men. *The Continual Pilgrimage: American Writers in Paris, 1944–1960* by Christopher Sawyer-Lauçanno (Grove Press and Bloomsbury, 1992) gives lively information not only about Richard Wright, James Baldwin and Chester Himes but also about such white American writers as James Jones, Irwin Shaw and John Ashbery. I read (and reviewed at the time) Frank McShane's *Into Eternity: The Life of James Jones, American Writer* (Houghton Mifflin, 1985). *The Last Avant-Garde* by David Lehman has a good chapter on John Ashbery in Paris.

I read several biographies of African American artists, including *Sidney Bechet: The Wizard of Jazz* by John Chilton (Da Capo, 1996); *My Life of Absurdity: The Later Years*, the second volume of the autobiography of Chester Himes

(Paragon, 1976); and two biographies of Josephine Baker, *Jazz Cleopatra* by Phyllis Rose (Doubleday and Chatto & Windus, 1989) and *Josephine: The Hungry Heart* by Jean-Claude Baker (her adopted son) and Chris Chase (Random House, 1993).

For the section about Jews in France I consulted *Les Juifs de France de la Révolution française à nos jours,* essays edited by Jean-Jacques Becker and Annette Wieviorka (Liana Lévi, 1998), and *The Jews of Modern France* by Paula E. Hyman (California, 1998). For the Jewish Marais I looked at *Je me souviens du Marais* by Bernadette Costa (Parigramme, 1995) and especially *Rue des Rosiers: une manière d'être juif* by Jeanne Brody (Autrement, 1995). For details about the Camondo family I read *Les Camondo ou l'éclipse d'une fortune* by Nora Seni and Sophie Le Tarnec (Actes Sud Hébraïca, 1997) and *Le dernier des Camondo* by Pierre Assouline (a well-known journalist and the biographer of Gaston Gallimard). The Camondo book was published by Gallimard in 1997. Finally, I studied the catalogue of the Nissim de Camondo Museum by Nadine Gasc and Gérard Mabillé (Fondation Paribas, 1997).

Edmund White

In writing about Baudelaire and the Hôtel Lauzun I looked at the beautifully illustrated *L'Île
Saint-Louis* (Action Artistique de la ville de Paris,
1997), which has an excellent essay on the *hôtel*
by Marie-Hélène Bersani. I read *Les Maisons du
Génie* by Claude Arthaud (Arthaud, 1967);
L'Histoire, la vie, les moeurs et la curiosité,
vol. 5 (Librairie de la Curiosité, 1928); *Demeures
inspirées et sites romanesques*, vol. 2, by Ray-
mond Lécuyer (Les Editions de l'Illustration, no
date). I found delightful Jean Ziegler's *Gautier-
Baudelaire: Un carré de dames* (Nizet, 1978). I
quote Théophile Gautier's 'Le Club des Hachichins', reprinted in his *Oeuvres* (Laffont, 1995). I
used Eugène Crépet's *Charles Baudelaire* (Léon
Vaniel, 1993) and I quote from Théodore de
Banville's *Mes Souvenirs* (Charpentier, 1882). I
also looked at *Les Ecrivains de l'Île Saint-Louis*
(Le Promeneur des Lettres, no date and no
author).

In my rather unfair discussion of Gustave
Moreau I learned from (but seldom agreed with)
such masterful studies as Geneviève Lacambre's
Gustave Moreau: Between Epic and Dream (Art
Institute of Chicago, 1999), the catalogue for the
show that started in Paris and travelled to Chicago and the Metropolitan in New York. *Gustave Moreau* by Pierre-Louis Mathieu

(Flammarion, 1994) is also a handsome tribute. I found more anecdotes to catch my eye in an earlier, less elegant book, *Tout l'Oeuvre peint de Gustave Moreau* by the same Mathieu (Flammarion, 1991; published in English by ACR Editions, 1998). I discovered a few useful details in *Gustave Moreau: Magic and Symbols* by the aforementioned Geneviève Lacambre, a little Gallimard book translated into English and printed in the Harry Abrams Discoveries series (1999). I found myself in close agreement with the assessment of Moreau in Victor Segalen's *Gustave Moreau, maître imagier de l'Orphisme,* a short, pithy study reprinted and introduced by the ubiquitous Mathieu in 1984 (Fata Morgana). *Manet's Modernism, or The Face of Painting in the 1860s* by Michael Fried (University of Chicago, 1996) has a telling comparison of Moreau's *Oedipus* with Manet's work.

For the chapter on homosexuality I consulted a biographical dictionary, *Homosexuels et bisexuels célèbres* by Michel Larivière (Deletraz Editions, 1997), a rather frivolous but amusing book. *Les bûchers de Sodome* by Maurice Lever (Fayard, 1985) is also amusing, and it is at the same time a treasure trove of lore about the persecution of homosexuality from ancient Rome until today. *Homosexuality in Modern France*, edited by Jeffrey Merrick and Bryant T. Ragan, Jr (Oxford, 1996), is a brilliant collection of essays about the fate of homosexuality from the Enlightenment up to our day, with a special emphasis on the formation of subcultures, popular attitudes, politics and the law. *A Taste for Freedom: The Life of Astolphe de Custine* is a gracefully written biography by Anka Muhlstein (English-language edition by Helen Marx Books, 1999); this is the best account of the openly gay aristocrat who befriended Chopin and wrote a classic study of Russia. I found interesting and relevant material about Custine in *Chopin in Paris* by Tad Szulc (Da Capo, 1998).

I mention the invaluable *Spartacus International Gay Guide*, which is published every year by Bruno Gmünder, Berlin, in a multilingual edition.

Anyone interested in lesbian and gay studies in France should write for the catalogue of the many excellent studies published or reprinted by Patrick Cardon: Cahiers GKC Boite Postale 36, 59009 Lille Cedex, France. He has reprinted many 'curiosa' such as *Pédérastie Active* (1907) and its companion piece *Pédérastie Passive: Mémoires d'un enculé* (1911). There is a whole series of reprints devoted to *Libertins* (a

The Flâneur

typical title is *Les Infames sous l'ancien régime*). There are even quite up-to-date studies, such as the one on *Back-rooms* by Rommel Mendès-Leite and Pierre-Olivier de Busscher.

The drag balls of the twenties are well documented in *Paris Gay 1925*, interviews with survivors of that period conducted by Gilles Barbedette and Michel Carassou (Presses de la Renaissance, 1981).

The late 1970s, early 1980s nightlife is covered in *Les Années Palace* by Daniel Garcia (Flammarion, 1999). The Palace was the French counterpart to Studio 54 in New York.

Contemporary debates over gay identity politics and AIDS are invoked in *Le Rose et le noir: Les homosexuels en France depuis 1968* (Seuil, 1996) and *Réflexions sur la question gay* by Didier Eribon (Fayard, 1999) as well as *Act Up: une histoire* by Didier Lestrade, the founder (Denoël, 2000).

For the chapter about royalists I read *La Basilique de Saint-Denis* by Branislav Brankovic, which is sold at the cathedral-basilica. The Chapelle Expiatoire is covered in *Paris* by Louis Hautecoeur, vol. 2, 1715–1972 (published by Fernand Nathan in 1972). I found additional information in the *Dictionnaire historique des rues de Paris* by Jacques Hillairet (two volumes, Editions de Minuit, 1985) in the entries under 'Place de la Concorde' and 'Square Louis XVI'. *Action Française* by Eugen Weber (Stanford University Press, 1962) covers the period from the foundation of the AF to the Liberation. *Histoire des Royalistes de la Libération à nos jours* by Patrick Louis (Jacques Grancher, 1994) sums up the current state of royalism as 'a nebulous cloud of little groups'. *De la Place Louis XV à la Place de la Concorde*, a 1982 catalogue for an exhibition at the Musée Carnavalet (the museum of the history of the city of Paris), gives a detailed account of contemporary representations of the beheading of Louis XVI.

Henri, the Count of Paris, wrote two useful books: *Mon Album de famille* (Club France Loisirs/Editions Perrin, 1997), which covers the history of the Orléans family from the time of Louis Philippe to 1950; and *Mémoires d'exil et de combats* (Atelier Marcel Jullian, 1979), which is a personal and 'dynastic' autobiography. When the Count of Paris died, there was extensive coverage of his entire life and career in the French press, especially in *Le Monde* (22 June 1999), twenty-four adulatory pages in *Point de Vue* (23–29 June 1999) and in *Paris Match* (twenty-eight pages in the 1 July 1999 issue). The scandal of the missing fortune was revealed in *L'Express* on 26 August 1999.

Thierry Ardisson, a popular television personality, came out in favour of Louis XX, the Duc d'Anjou, in *Louis XX: Contre-enquête sur la monarchie* (Editions Olivier Orban, 1986). The Institut de la Maison de Bourbon published a pamphlet recently (no date given), *France, que fais-tu de ton histoire?* (the title is an allusion to the question Pope John-Paul II asked when he first visited France, *'France, qu'as-tu fait de ton baptême?'*). This pamphlet serves up some rather dishy photos of the current Bourbon pretender to the throne and a potted history of his family.

At the Bar-Tabac des Templiers I was sold some handouts about the false claims of the Orleanists ('Les Prétendus Orléans: Depuis le frère de Louis XIV, il n'y a plus d'Orléans' was the title of one, and another, without title, presented the programme of this particular group). Yet another, titled 'Ordre', announces that 'the natural hierarchy' consists of 'children, parents, family, clan, Nation, King, Church and Christ', an order that is 'Divine because Natural, the work of God. All Order should be the Guarantee of the Divine Hierarchy, under the Patronage of the Virgin Mary in the love of Christ.'

There are thousands of novels about Paris, old and new. The few that happen to be talismanic for me include, of course, Proust's *In Search of Lost Time* (or, as it used to be called, *Remembrance of Things Past*; translated by Scott Moncrieff and Terence Kilmartin, Vintage, 1996). This is a book that shows the anatomy and the physiology of Paris in the Belle Époque and embraces everything from a description of famous beauties promenading in the Bois de Boulogne to a learned but lighthearted account of vendors' cries. Amid the classics, such as Eugène Sue's *Les Mystères de Paris* and Victor Hugo's *Les Misérables* (translated 1901 by Norman Denny, Penguin, 1982), I especially like Balzac's novel sequence *Illusions perdues* (translated by Kathleen Raine as *Lost Illusions*, Modern Library, 1997) and *Splendeurs et misères des courtisanes* (translated by Rayner Heppenstall as *A Harlot High and Low*, Penguin, 1970). Oscar Wilde once said that the saddest moment of his life was the death of Lucien de Rubempré, the young, vain, foolish and touching hero of these two novels, which tell the reader everything she or he needs to know about how young people from the provinces exploit (and are exploited by) the older, richer people they meet in the capital. Flaubert's *Sentimental Education* (translated by

Robert Baldick, Penguin, 1970) is also about a provincial's success and ultimate failure in the Paris of 1848. But the subject of the ambitious young man 'mounting' to Paris is an inexhaustible theme – Alphonse Daudet's autobiographical *Le petit Chose* is one of the most successful (and sentimental) examples of the genre. Emile Zola, patterning his work after Balzac's *La Comédie humaine*, wrote books that followed a programme. For instance, he showed the poor of Paris in *L'Assommoir* (translated by Margaret Mauldon, OUP, 1999), the underworld of prostitutes in *Nana* (translated by Douglas Parmée, OUP, 1998), and the destructive power of Haussmannian Paris in *La Curée*.

Among twentieth-century novels and nonfiction books, Colette's *Chéri* and *The Last of Chéri* (translated by Roger Senhouse, Penguin, 1990, in one volume) are unforgettable renderings of the demimonde before and after the First World War; the sophistication and sensuality of these novels are true emanations of the spirit of Paris. Ernest Hemingway's *A Moveable Feast* (Arrow, 1994) is a rich evocation of Paris in the twenties, a period when a flock of goats might still trot down the rue Mouffetard at dawn to provide fresh milk to customers who'd lower pails from windows. No one could forget Hemingway's story of how he threaded his way around the Left Bank in order to avoid going past tempting bakeries and greengrocers and restaurants at a time when he was broke and hungry.

Simone de Beauvoir has written beautifully about Paris in all the phases of her life as child, student, intellectual, feminist and companion to Sartre in such books as *The Prime of Life*, *Force of Circumstances* (Marlowe & Co., 1992), *The Mandarins* (W. W. Norton & Co., 1999), *Memoirs of a Dutiful Daughter* (translated by James Kirkup, Penguin, 1990) and *The Coming of Age* (translated by Patrick O'Brien, W. W. Norton & Co., 1996).

André Gide's *The Counterfeiters* (Penguin, 1990) is his best novel, and one in which Paris is ever present as a character. The neurotic happenings of Drieu la Rochelle's *Le Feu follet* (*The Fire Within*) take place against a familiar Paris backdrop. Elizabeth Bowen's *The House in Paris* (Vintage, 1998) is a masterpiece of narrative art that plays Paris off against Cork and the past against the present. James Baldwin's *Giovanni's Room* (Penguin, 2000) is not only a gay classic but also a portrait of the Paris of the 1950s.

My own *The Married Man* (Chatto & Windus, 2000) can be read as a paean to contemporary Paris. Juan Goytisolo's *Landscape After the Bat-*

tle (translated by Helen Lane, Serpent's Tail, 1987) is an avant-garde novel about multicultural Paris. Matthew Stadler's *Allan Stein* (Fourth Estate, 1999) is partly an imaginary biography of Gertrude Stein's nobody nephew and partly the record of a modern love affair in Paris today. Peter Gadol's *Light at Dusk* (Picador USA, 2000) imagines a Paris that has been taken over by the racist far right, a place where biracial children are kidnapped and the boulevards are given over to fires and rioting crowds.

A NOTE ON THE AUTHOR

The author of many books including *A Boy's Own Story* and most recently *The Married Man*, Edmund White has been made an officer in the French Order of Arts and Letters and last year received a literary prize from the Festival of Deauville. Ten of his books have been translated into French, including his magisterial biography of Jean Genet.

A NOTE ON THE TYPE

The text of this book is set in Linotype
Sabon, named after the type founder, Jacques
Sabon. It was designed by Jan Tschichold
and jointly developed by Linotype, Monotype
and Stempel, in response to a need for a
typeface to be available in identical form for
mechanical hot metal composition and hand
composition using foundry type.

Tschichold based his design for Sabon roman
on a fount engraved by Garamond, and
Sabon italic on a fount by Granjon. It was
first used in 1966 and has proved an
enduring modern classic.